PS
3515   Hough, Henry Beetle
.075933
Z52   To the Harbor
            Light

DATE DUE

APR 5 78			

TO THE

Henry Beetle Hough

TO THE

HARBOR LIGHT

Drawings by Donald Carrick

HOUGHTON MIFFLIN COMPANY BOSTON 1976

Library of Congress Cataloging in Publication Data

Hough, Henry Beetle, date
  To the Harbor Light.

  1. Hough, Henry Beetle, 1896–   —Biography.
I. Title.
PS3515.075933Z52   070.4'092'4 [B]   76-20534
ISBN 0-395-24774-8

Printed in the United States of America

v 10 9 8 7 6 5 4 3 2 1

To E. G. B.

TO THE HARBOR LIGHT

ONE OF THE THINGS that had concerned me lately was whether or not I was a normal baby. Perhaps it couldn't matter anymore — or could it? Anyone who reads the newspapers nowadays knows the importance of being or of having been a normal baby, an importance that runs without limit and the requirements of which become stricter as additional findings are published. I am reasonably sure that few of these requirements could have been fulfilled in my case, way back four years before the turn of the century.

Among the photographs I brought down from the attic are a few that show me in infancy, though I could not have separated them out from a mixture of unidentifiable baby pictures, most of which I take to portray my ancestors, if my father had not written my name on the back of each in his positive editorial script. All babies leave me, to say the least, unmoved; and I recall the opinion of a seafaring uncle by marriage who said they should be kept in a barrel and fed through the bunghole until ready to emerge in human form. At any rate, it may be said that I possessed a high, nicely rounded forehead and dark eyes capable of being astonished at the goings-on in the yonder world.

It wasn't a large world at the time. The scrolled end of a brown upholstered couch that I remember even now tells me that the photographer came to 85 Campbell Street to preserve the baby likenesses of my brother and myself. He mounted us on stiff polite cardboard with crimped gilt edges, imprinted at the bottom with professional flourishes, "O'Neil, New Bedford."

I was a victim of the fashion of long baby dresses, though whoever had to launder those dresses must have been the greater sufferer by far. Here I see myself as Mr. O'Neil posed me, small hands barely and helplessly protruding from the sleeves of that improbable garment, which, since it reached the floor and I was positioned at the elevation of a table top, must have been at least thirty inches longer than my dangling legs.

The hair that was to cover a proper part of my head, though temporarily as it proved, appears tentatively as a slight fuzz. So far, so good, I might be tempted to say. If there is nothing to give me any real measure in today's scale of normality, at least there is no indication of the uncertainty with which I was to traverse the risky way ahead. I see myself as a barely existent though apparently complete beginner, assured of nothing, open to all the chances, enigmas, hopes, and sins lying ahead in a new cataclysmic century.

This had been my thought when an unexpected confrontation returned me to the present moment. So often are extremes, black and white, youth and age, balanced off by the chance of a moment, or brought together in unlikely or ironic synchronism. My baby pictures were on my desk, and so now is a newly arrived letter from the editor of *Who's Who in America*, who proposes an epilogue for me as a man of completed life.

Though he is dropping me from the forthcoming volume of *Who's Who* — this is delicately put: I am transferred to a "non-current category" — he will include me in "the comprehensive coverage provided by our companion publication, *Who's Who in American History* (sixth volume now in compilation)."

I suspect the presence of some mocking laughter in the realm of the destiny that surrounds us all. Is the jest upon the baby in the picture, on me, or on American history?

The editor goes beyond his reasonable prerogatives, brushing past the fact that history has intentions and surprises of its own. There is the prospect of years during which the sixth volume will have been succeeded by a sixtieth, a seventieth, a hundredth, and so on; and what will really remain is that image of myself, the infant in the long dress, peering out with the astonishment that adults have the misfortune to outgrow. Something elusive hangs in the air, turn it this way or that as you please to catch the light.

I need only fill out a form as to this baby's — or my — further activities and "any significant development" for his — or my — or our — name to go into a great red-covered book, Volume Six. But I don't know what significance is, though once I thought I did. I'll wait a while before deciding. There's a great deal that needs thinking over.

∽

Graham is waiting for me now. He is my collie and companion, three years old this month, and we live alone.

Betty, who was my wife for forty-five years, died in 1965, and Lochinvar, the last collie we owned together, survived only until October 22, 1971, a day I remember clearly.

"This is a cool October morning," I wrote in the erratic journal I was attempting to keep, "so like the late October mornings of Martha's Vineyard. It is the morning of Lochinvar's execution, for his helplessness is too far advanced already. He is old and sad and needs help to raise his hind legs from the ground. The temperature dropped last night into the low forties, but now the sun is well up and its warmth drifts through the crisp, cool air. The mist over Sheriff's Meadow Pond, a white reek, has risen so that it forms a straight horizontal line at the tops of the pine trees. But now it lowers again and hides the pond.

"We were up a little before six and breakfast was as usual, except that Lochinvar had more to eat. We fed the birds, took the weather readings, and went to the office; a few proofs to read, a bag to take out and throw away. Lochinvar stayed in the car. This has been his imprisonment for months past. Tom Van Howe came in, and then Don MacPhee. No last minute news from Joe.

"We came home and I offered to take Lochinvar for a walk. He did not want to go. He has confessed his weakness to himself. I cleaned the lower hall for the last time, and for the last time put back the braided rug.

"It is now 8:10 and I am going down to give Lochinvar his sleeping pills. His final memory, if any memories remain, will be of his master giving him something pleasant to eat. And things to eat are his last interest, the final measure of capabilities diminished day by day for so long . . .

"I have given Lochinvar his barbiturates and said good-by to him, and told him that his master and mistress loved him. He couldn't hear, but he has always known."

So then I took him in my arms and drove to the shelter of the S.P.C.A. to have them do what had to be done. A dog's life is so much shorter than a man's, and Lochinvar was eleven.

◌

Long experience had taught me that I needed a dog; the open land and shore, the country seasons demand a large dog, and a collie is just right. So it was Graham I brought home from the Cape at the age of a few weeks, a downy pup with white muzzle and a thin white blaze on his forehead, given to crossing his legs as he walked or stood, and with an endless interest in all the natural and human worlds around him.

I needed him for companionship and to make sounds in the house at night. I needed him for the walks we were to take each morning all year to the lighthouse at the end of the causeway. We stand there as the sun appears, a red ball in a red-orange sky.

Attending to the sequence of divine events, I could make myself aware of the turning of the earth toward the sun, our stationary star and lamp. I could feel myself a passenger upon the bending rim, so slowly being advanced along with Graham, a great blue heron in the lagoon, and the gulls atop the wharf spiles; or, more aptly, as again a sightseer of recurring dawns. Once the red rim of the sun became visible, our motion toward it seemed to undergo a quickening. The close prelude to what we call sunrise gave way to a rapid fulfillment. Up, up it seemed to come — swiftly up now, and the roofs and treetops of the town were gilded as Graham and I walked back along the causeway.

The sun appeared well to the north of the lighthouse, and before the end of December it will appear well to the south, at the foot of Main Street, so that anyone going down the street will see it face to face. Our traveling earth will have taken us to the north and we will say by habit that the sun has moved toward the south.

⌣

Graham was named for all the Scottish Grahams, some in Betty's family, some in Edie Blake's, for she, herself a Graham, will look after him if he survives his master. He is named too, I suppose, for Graham of Claverhouse, mortally wounded at Killiekrankie, known also as Bonnie Dundee or Bloody Claverse. There's also Graham of Montrose, who in the end was captured and hanged, to live all the longer in Scottish romance. But you give a dog a name you like and he becomes in your life what you want him to be.

He and I combine two different worlds, and I draw upon his youth to make me younger in action and outlook than I would otherwise be. A man approaching eighty is on dangerous ground and is likely to think too much apart.

Has he not lived in an age of magnificence, now gone, such as no one now living or in future to be born can experience? He becomes his own Charles de Gaulle, filling out the symbolism of that tall, ungainly frame, with an unswerving conviction of destiny. The greatness of the past is viewed each day in relation to the degraded present, and the little contemporary men in their unawareness contribute to the de Gaullean proportion of the spirit that flourished under a better sun and in better times. How can the present be so blind?

It is not by accident that a Gallic metaphor and impersonation are suggested here, for in the New England in which I have lived and which I truly know, there is hardly an alternative other than a furtive sense of having been conspired against, which, difficult of concealment, leads one's neighbors to say one has "turned queer." In age a man may become a stranger in his native land and is best advised to secure himself with the bravest fantasies.

The past itself is purpled and gilded. The times were braver than we thought, and like a de Gaulle we can look upon defeats and lost causes as a particular merit. We need confide in no one. Our self-knowledge is glowing and complete — also safely away from the light of another day.

Age is an absolute on a fading afternoon.

A more usual expression is, "What the hell did any of it matter?" Yes, any of us can say that, too, but the de Gaulle is nevertheless close behind our shoulders.

～

I fell in yesterday with my neighbor, Milton Birch, and we walked along our lane together, not hurrying at all in the warm morning sunlight. We both live alone, according to the town's opinion, but he has no dog, and this accounts for a great difference.

"I've just hung out my wash on the line," Milton said. "Only a few people have clotheslines any more, but I don't like a dryer. If you dry your wash outdoors it smells entirely different. Did you ever dry any wash on Chappaquiddick?"

"No," I said.

"Well, I don't suppose you ever had occasion to. But it smells entirely different over there. When the wild roses are blooming and the breeze comes fresh over the water and then across those fields it goes all through the clothes on the line and they smell wonderful."

I do have a clothesline but until recently my front yard, very wide and deep, retaining much character of the open field it used to be, was heavily shaded by giant elms and inefficient for drying. The other day I lost the two forward

elms and, though they lacked the monumental majesty of
the two at the east of the house, I will mourn them as long
as I live. They had contracted Dutch elm disease. One had
seemed convalescent after Dick Mansfield gave it injections
of a new fungicide last summer and again this spring. The
initial wilt was cut away, the tree revived, and the new
foliage in May and June rejoiced me and all passers-by.
But then the wilt came again and swiftly had its way.

According to the growth rings, fifty years had passed
since I planted those two elms, slender poles needing support against the wind. Betty was all for putting out trees
at once, as soon as the land was ours, a pasture lot gone wild
with a rim of thicket and briars. The uneven surface
dipped nicely into a hollow through which a stream used
to flow from a place near the Methodist Church a quarter of
a mile away. I imagine a good part of the town was drained
through what became our yard. The stream still flows but
underground and slowly, until it empties at last into
Sheriff's Meadow Pond. Betty did not think that anyone
should stop planting elms, no matter what the threat, and
of course she was right. The elms deserved their chance
against the Dutch invader.

No one could know then, venturing an act of faith, that
in fifty years a wiry, red-headed foreman would come with
a gang of men and a boy, and a hundred thousand dollars'
worth of equipment, to begin way up aloft and take down
those two front elms for removal to the dump. The equipment, which gained access to the front yard by the removal
of the fence beside the mulberry tree, consisted of three
huge trucks, two with lofty cranes and one with a sturdy,
ordinary orange-peel hoist capable of loading great weights
of logs and branches into its truck body.

One man soared in a self-controlled bucket and attached
a rope to an uppermost spreading elm branch; then, while

the red-headed foreman made that rope taut, he descended to a lower level and cut through a manageable segment of the tree with a chain saw. The chain saws rasped and disagreeably chanted, hour after hour, cutting, cutting, cutting.

I did not take the death of the elms as the result of any act of nature. I blamed it, correctly, on the deadly advance of communication and transportation in this ill-starred age. The story is an old one, going back to the Crusades, the voyages of Captain Cook, stout Cortez, and others, and no doubt of captains such as Valentine Pease of Edgartown, who was master of the *Acushnet* when Herman Melville sailed on her as a foremast hand. The disease and death of one part of the world are now shared liberally with all other parts. Even more unfortunate than the loss of the elms is the effect of too much communication on the human race. The modern age does to human beings what it does to trees in a general way, but its agents in our case are not so obvious as the elm bark beetle.

I have two elms left, at least for the time being, the mightiest and most beautiful, at the side of the house toward the east or a little to the southeast, but my premises no longer have the unstudied symmetry brought about by Betty when she said, "Let's put them there — and there — and there — not too near the house. We want to keep the southern sunlight for the winter." There's plenty of space now for air and sunlight. I'd call it a void.

"Don't you like having the sun again?" asks a passer-by.

I don't, of course. I liked the old, slowly achieved shade and what more than one visitor spoke of as a "southern look." It was a southern look, too. I liked not having to cut the grass, which wouldn't grow without more than a dappling of sunlight. I even liked the green, mouldy moss.

I might now have rose borders again where they grew so

well before World War II, when the front walk was still sunny. But I don't think so. My energies incline to shorter and easier tasks, and my rose phase stands in my mind as completed. Besides, the roses we liked best are hard to find. Where now are Betty Uprichard, Copper Glow, Golden Climber, or even Etoile de Hollande? The very rose growers from whom we bought them in former days are gone.

So the sunny spaces in front of the house will remain, and after my conversation with Milton Birch I think I will arrange to hang my wash there. I toy with the notion of two clotheslines bordering the path to the mulberry tree and the gate, my undershirts on one, my shorts on the other.

The air in our part of town is sweet at any time of year, even if not so sweet as the summer air of Chappaquiddick, and I think my semiweekly wash should come back to me with a tang of the natural seasons and times of day. Come to think of it, I have been meaning to put out a whole hedge of swamp honeysuckle and sweet pepperbush for all-summer fragrance. The question is, will I ever get to it?

Come to think of it also, I was compelled the other day to buy some furiously striped shorts instead of the plain white ones I prefer. My clothesline can be really gay, which is excellent if passers-by don't misread the pageantry as a sign of my character.

The elms and shade had more to say more truthfully than any wash swaying from a line, though the latter, if not too decorative, will also fall neatly into the New England tradition.

∽

Mornings should begin as eagerly as this one did. Use of the adjective "eagerly" involves a figure of speech, of course, as well as Ruskin's pathetic fallacy — which he himself continued to employ after he had exposed it. The figure would be metonymy, naming of effect for cause: my own eagerness and Graham's for the bright clear sunlight and inspiriting northwest wind across the harbor, and the temperature of 52 degrees. When I studied Shakespeare in the New Bedford High School under Miss Lydia J. Cranston, who had instructed my father at an earlier period with similar dissatisfaction, she would have us read assigned passages aloud and at intervals would call out abruptly, "Figure!" This meant that she and all of us had encountered the arresting phenomenon of synecodoche, enallage, metonymy, and so on. That was how English literature was taught.

Figure of speech or no, it was eagerly that Graham and I walked to the lighthouse, and eager the whole morning seemed to us. His sniffing muzzle, alert eyes and ears showed how he was taking the experience. He keened into the wind and the approaching dawn, a delightful realization of life in his nostrils, so much more knowing than mine. I envied the naturalness with which he turned excitement into satisfaction.

We had left the house in a moderately lessened darkness, the edge of daylight creeping around us. We walked to the turn of Pease's Point Way, that old, simple, and becoming street, and down the country lane to the Johnson house, then across Bob Brown's moor where a wildness of marsh was combined, autumn fashion, with meadow — sedges, white and purple asters, goldenrod, evening primroses, and so many tatters of old summer. Graham chose his moment to roll, writhing vigorously on his back, feet in the air so that I could see them above the thatch of russet grasses. His legs are always white and clean.

The eastern sky had reddened into a cool, lavish display with hues of pink and blood-orange. The air was still, parting gently around us as we made a triple turn and emerged in front of the Harbor View, a crazy old hotel standing in a pride of piazzas, gables, and upturned rocking chairs, commanding the noblest of outlooks. We had met no one. We walked the length of the causeway and stood beside the lighthouse while the sky was drained of its color.

∽

A gull flew over from Chappaquiddick, followed by others now ready for day, choosing their spile-tops gracefully. The first man-made sound was that of the Chappaquiddick ferry, then a fishing boat started in the inner harbor and passed swiftly by with twin furrows which spread into smooth waves, rocking other boats at their moorings. Ripples came to the shore, and a whiff of breeze crossed the harbor and was lost before another had begun.

Our earth turned and we inclined with it. I watched the sky, and Graham eyed casually a great blue heron standing motionless where the sedge met the lagoon. Nothing can be more motionless (for there are degrees even in that state) than a great blue heron standing sentinel. He exudes poised quietude, not like a statue which is of necessity forever graven. Now the color returned to the sky and I could see where the sun would be disclosed — and there it was, a rim, an arc, and all of a sudden it had "come up."

We turned from the sudden flood of clear light and walked back along the causeway, watching the glow caught in the windows of the town, gilding rooflines and chimneys. We had, though not precisely by the almanac, watched October arrive. On North Water Street a man in shorts, gray-haired, with his wife, each carrying a fishing pole, said good morning, and all our faces were tinted by October's sun.

In Sheriff's Lane, as we turned into the final stretch toward home, there was no darkness but no real daylight either, just the twinkling of the sun's new rays in the leaves of the trees overhead, and the remoter effulgence on the far side of Sheriff's Meadow Pond where the dawn already reached cleanly across the water. "Effulgence" — I wonder if that's too fancy a word? When I was in high school I was advised along with the rest of my class to learn one new word from the dictionary every day. One day I learned "coruscations" and no one would let me use it. Disillusioned, I decided to let the dictionary alone except in emergencies.

Our lighthouse at the end of the causeway on the channel at the harbor entrance is quite different from Virginia Woolf's, so fascinatingly far at sea. We go afoot to it every morning, and sometimes once or twice more in a day.

I was slow in reading Virginia Woolf's book. It was hard for me to get into. I would read a few pages, feel myself lost, and turn back to find out what had happened. Nothing had happened. But in a hospital room, recovering from a hernia operation, I made a companion of *To the Lighthouse* and came to love it well — the beauty of Mrs. Ramsay, the sad sweet-stormy passing of time, the painting problems of Lily Briscoe, Mr. Ramsay and his quotations as he paced the grounds, headlong and self-heroic, especially his "But I beneath a rougher sea was whelmed in deeper gulfs than he."

Virginia Woolf wrote that the lighthouse of her book had no particular symbolism. A friend to whom I mentioned this retorted, "It has, though!" How could my friend know better than Virginia Woolf herself? Well, of course it was possible. Everybody knows best.

Hiram Haydn asked me about the symbolism of a sailors' free reading room I had introduced into my novel *The*

Port. I had been afraid he would ask that, and I had no easy reply. The reading room had just come along naturally from a boyhood association, and there it was, stand or fall. I have since decided that the symbolism least contrived is closest to the genuine thing. Made-up symbols don't function well and are quickly outdistanced by time and the next one.

As to Virginia Woolf, I did find a good answer in *The Reader's Encyclopedia* — "the lighthouse, everyone's goal, symbolizes many things to many people." Now I know why, though Graham and I may walk a thousand times to the Harbor Light, our fixed purpose will be to go again. And often I look at distant Cape Pogue and its farthermost of Vineyard lighthouses, wondering if that is really the one, and my life is falling short. Once in the bitter February of 1933, when the harbor and bay were frozen, I did walk to Cape Pogue over the rough ice. I think the outer harbor will never freeze again in my time, and even if it should, I wonder if I am equal to the same adventure.

At any rate, the Harbor Light is ours to go to, and some of the attainment is always waiting for tomorrow. What I should like best, and something widely out of reason, would be a meeting on the causeway some summer or autumn morning with a girl named Minta Doyle eating a sandwich, or Lily Briscoe painting and slowly and at last getting that line on her canvas just right, maybe not in the center this time, but breathlessly where she wants it.

⌒

Graham ate a whole banana today. Should I have allowed him to do it? I not only allowed him, I peeled the banana and held it while he bit off pieces sidewise, munching them with more consideration than he gives to most of his food. He is an instant eater, or at times an instant abstainer. He knows what he likes, including bananas.

In my association with Graham, extending over almost three years now, I have avoided the clichés of modern education. I think I have been permissive enough for the modernists, but his social adjustment has concerned me not at all. Up in the red brick schoolhouse they can look after the herd, and a hell of a herd it is, but Graham and I are answerable only to ourselves. We have an understanding valid between individuals, complete, based on the unthinkable fact that either without the other would be living in a great desert of solitude. Social studies are not concerned with such as us, heretically separated out. We have an unorthodox insulation around us, mostly constituted of fresh air.

When Graham comes loping across a field, full tilt, and flings himself at me, all four feet in the air, brushing my cheek and usually my glasses with his tongue as he flies past, friends or observing strangers say to me, "Do you know how to break him of that?" They are much too ready to tell me, and usually I cannot choke them off, though I think I have known as long as they. Graham is as agile as a circus dancer, as accurate, and as delicate. I encourage his personality and his humor, for that is at the heart of his springings and loping assaults. He also throws himself up and at me when I sneeze, a custom he formed when he was a puppy. It is hardly safe for anyone to sneeze in his presence, but his objects so far have suffered from nothing worse than astonishment, and I think some sneezers have been cured or reformed.

Only the other day I realized that I had never administered corporal punishment or discipline to Graham except once when I slapped his flank smartly to admonish him out of the way of an automobile. He was surprised at first but then understood perfectly, as he assured me with his eyes and tail.

I have required nothing more of him than to be house-broken and not to beg at table, an easy minimum which is also an easy maximum. Whether he can shake hands is a matter of indifference to me, and anyway I see no sense in the command, "Give me your paw." He always has more use for his paw than I have.

Housebreaking, so great a burden to many dogs and dog-owners, did not trouble Graham and me except briefly. The importance lay in attending to him closely for the first day or two, putting him outdoors immediately after his frequent puppy meals and so often otherwise that he couldn't make what is euphemistically called a "mistake" inside the house.

Graham mastered the housebreaking idea so well that soon he observed the hygienic security not only of the house but of the whole large yard and contiguous neighborhood, insisting that he must go always yonder for evacuation. Some of his favorite places are pretty far from where we live, and occasionally we put on speed to get there in time. Once in a while he and I go all the way to the lighthouse causeway for his determined purpose.

Of course I remember the story I heard as a small boy, hilarious in its day, about an elderly couple in England who planned to take in a lodger. One applicant wrote to ask how far the W.C. was from the house. The old people puzzled a while and decided the inquirer meant "Wesleyan Chapel," so they wrote back that it was half a mile.

I feel that I have time to take Graham where he wants to go, though neither of us has enough time overall, within our earthly allotment.

◠

I knew Old Tom Baylies who lived with his dog Shep in a small house he had built at the edge of town. What I wrote about him long ago is as vivid to me today as ever. I thought of Old Tom walking down Main Street in the shrilling autumn with the orange glow of a cold twilight behind him, a scurrying wind whipping an immense double-breasted coat, a scarf knotted about his throat, and a gold-headed cane in the grip of his long, mottled fingers. There was much of the venerable squire about Old Tom, and I think of him now with his dog, good mongrel Shep, who should have been a collie or a wolfhound.

Old Tom should have walked as I describe him now, glaring sternly at the town children, lifting his furzy eyebrows and grimacing under his white mustachios to conceal the amiability of his mellow heart — Old Tom, the patriarch, in thriving autumnal days. But I do not really remember him so, for he never carried a gold-headed cane and his imagined great coat is one he never wore. In the strict account of memory there is only the knotted scarf, though I am fairly sure of a shiny blue serge jacket.

Tom Baylies had a distinguished bearing because that was his birthright and represented the period and the family from which he came, but he was neither judge, professor, nor senator. He was a carpenter, and in his youth he had taught many a younger man how to frame a house.

He was born in Edgartown, the son of a whaling master who commanded the gorgeously christened ships *Timoleon* and *Amethyst* and later went into the grocery business. The captain moved to Indiana to get away from the sea, invented and sold a new kind of baking powder. Young Tom saw homesteaders moving westward over wagon tracks in army escort wagons, flocks of passenger pigeons, and Quakers holding convention in a great pavilion. But it isn't easy to escape the sea, and his father brought the family home to Edgartown.

Tom made a voyage south on a mackerel schooner, then

stayed at home, learned his trade, and was good at it. "Ours was one of the first families," he said once, "and in my day when I was prosperous people used to call me Mr. Baylies. But now things are changed and I am just Old Tom Baylies to most of them. Still, I'm not complaining."

One evening Tom and Shep walked into the dining room of Hallowell's Restaurant on lower Main Street when it was pretty well filled with summer people. Old Tom gave his order and, after drumming on the table with his knuckles for a minute or two, recited to no one in particular:

> "There was a young lady of Niger
> Who smiled as she rode on a tiger . . ."

And so on to the end. Strangers stared at Old Tom but he paid no attention and was presently addressing his dinner with gusto.

Another time he flung open the door of the lunchroom side of the restaurant and strode in with Shep at his heels as if he were a commandant announced by bugles. He ordered coffee and doughnuts, and as soon as Mr. Hallowell put the doughnuts within reach, seized them and with a few brisk motions of his long fingers crumpled them into fragments which he flung upon the floor in a reckless scatter for Shep to retrieve and devour. He then sat on a stool at the counter, ignoring the baleful eye of Mr. Hallowell, and drank his coffee in style.

When he was well past eighty Old Tom had to go to a hospital. Shep went along in the car, and there was no objection to that. When the hospital doors closed upon his master, though, he was left outside. This was natural, too, but Shep watched his chance and slipped inside with some new arrival, nosing his way to the men's ward where Old Tom lay. Tom was not surprised.

"This is a hell of a place for a dog," remarked one of the other patients.

"Get under the bed," Tom said to Shep, and Shep did.

But of course the nurse found him in the morning and he was taken to the animal shelter run by Miss Kitty Foote. She knew from experience and general wisdom that Shep would not stay with her, so she took him to his own home and carried his meals to him regularly, serving him properly on his own premises. If he had wanted afternoon tea she would have served that, and gladly, for she was getting on to be as old as Tom.

In a few weeks Tom was discharged from the hospital, and he and Shep were reunited. All was well again, for a while.

"Shep doesn't like to sleep on my bed," Tom said, "but if I am sick he will get up on the bed and put his head right under my chin and cry."

There was a year of moderately good times and then Old Tom was hardly able to be left living alone. This was the humanitarian decision of the town, so the selectmen made arrangements for him to be boarded in a good household. The only trouble was that Tom and Shep preferred their own arrangements. During the night Tom climbed through a window, whistled to Shep, and they went home together, the master taking his long strides through the darkness, the dog trotting by his side.

There was talk of committing Tom to a state institution for his own good, where he might have the best of care, but nobody wanted to see that done. So once more he and Shep kept their fortress together. No enemies, or friends either, could get in, with the exception of old age and illness.

At last Tom was too ill to stay by himself, and this time, though he threatened a struggle, he went quietly, leaving

Shep and life — all of life that was worthwhile — behind him forever. The selectmen put Shep in the care of another old man who needed a dog and needed to be shown how to live alone. Shep taught him.

This is the story of Old Tom, and also the story of man, which will be found in the Bible and other ancient writings. So when I say there is plenty of time for Graham and me to walk to the lighthouse, I speak in a narrower frame of reference.

But there is this importance, too. After he was seventy-seven, Old Tom could still climb on roofs and nail shingles.

◇

In December 1971, I opened a long-unused bureau drawer and threw out all my city shirts, hoarded since 1926. Throwing out was clearly best for them and for me. I remembered strangely that I had been fond of one or two, I suppose because I thought I looked well in them. Youth has that kind of pride. Now they would make rags, though not the best rags, for Lillian and me to use in cleaning things around the house. Lillian comes twice a week to help with skillful and friendly care of the house. She began coming for two of us more than forty years ago, and now she comes for one.

This arrangement is important in the present and also because it secures me tautly to the past. A house needs its identity of habitation, yet I put beside this fact another that I have also tested for truth — the joy at last of arriving home and finding no one there.

It is not how you feel that matters — it is how old you are. This conflicts with a deceit that is much more popular, but realism at the end is required in any man's life.

I rise with a zest and eagerness on these brave October

mornings, the more so today with the wind blowing from the northeast. What is it that prompts these responses if not that unforgotten sense of vitality and youth? What else, indeed? I say to my doctor that I never felt more fit. Plans for the day surge into my mind and the tone of my muscles. What I plan, though, will not get done. For a while I could hide the truth of this, and even now I push it aside. I feel so well — cannot today be different? But it never is, for I am ruled by my age in years, and that's the truth and end of the matter.

Long ago when I woke in the morning, reluctant, listless, averse to all accumulated duties, I nevertheless worked diligently at the office for eight or nine hours and then trundled a wheelbarrow or dug in the garden until nightfall, and felt better for all this in the end. I was young then. Now I wake with refreshed and energetic spirit and accomplish little or nothing, because I am old. It may be that all signs fail sometimes in both youth and age. Expect the outcome and pay no serious attention to the barometer reading at the beginning of a new day.

A psychiatrist friend of Betty's and mine once wrote to a friend we knew well:

> I am learning first-hand a great deal about the problem of age. It has helped somewhat to recognize that it is one of those things and nothing can be done to stop it, and nothing really gained by denying it. That changes the problem to one of getting along with something which one cannot undo. It raises the question why anyone should be afraid of being old. I doubt if anyone is.
>
> You might get a clue if you stop to consider what it is you fear: such as the inability to keep going so fast as not to have to think; or the actual inability to do some things one could do a while ago; or the loss of the onward and upward incentive which is so strong in our culture, and the coinci-

dent discovery that what one has accomplished does not
measure up to one's intentions and ideals.

One of the most striking things about being older seems
to be the reduction in the ability to fantasize and in the
pleasure incident to fantasy. When this is recognized it is
unavoidable evidence that the self, or ego, or whatever you
call yourself, is losing some of its capabilities for pleasure.
I would guess much of the fear of aging is this general fear
of loss of aggressive function.

There are simple and practical things which help, such
as learning not to overdo physically, to accept the need for
more rest, for considerably less food, and to accept that it
is inevitable one will not be able to sleep his former quota
of hours, so that if he goes to bed early he will probably
wake up early. It becomes necessary to have some medical
supervision and to check on the beginnings of degenerative
diseases or malignancies and such, and this furnishes occasion to get advice on matters of diet, exercise and the rest
of it.

Sleep. The word brings up one general problem I share
with so many of my age — it is called "getting through the
night." The problem is somewhat mitigated for me when
I can rise early, but sleep remains elusive. So many of us
could easily become nocturnal, prowling through the night
and falling asleep at dawn to doze or languish all day.

I have received a lot of advice about sleeping. Wear
blinders. They have trade names but I don't recall. Move
from a bed in one room to a bed in another. Turn on the
light and read a book — but the book and my line of vision
never agree, and my hands and wrists become bloodless
from holding the book in position; or my neck cramps from
holding my head at a curiously difficult angle.

As to a nap in the middle of the day, it takes care of itself. I sit down to read a newspaper and fall asleep at once.

But if I go to bed for a nap I lie awake anxiously waiting for the time of release or getting up.

It was this same psychiatrist who, sitting under our elms one summer day, said that if the world were to be laid waste by war or the atomic bomb, within each human being still left alive would be a little grinning monster saying, "I survived!"

◇

In the same mail I have received both word of the Nostalgia Book Club and another invitation (the first arrived a year ago) from the American Association of Retired Persons. It is remarkable how popular old age has become. Or the aging and aged. I am being courted on the ground of my most recent birthday almost every week of the year, and if I am not careful some of these operators will get me yet. Insurance groups and good works will hardly take a refusal much longer.

The Association of Retired Persons offers a subscription to *Modern Maturity* — coals to Newcastle, I would think. I recall when my Aunt Emma, born in 1862, was being cared for at the Martha's Vineyard Hospital. Betty and I went to see her, and she told us mischievously that the nurse tried to keep her from eating with her fingers — but she ate with her fingers anyway. Whose side in such a case would the Association of Retired Persons and *Modern Maturity* support? I hope they wouldn't want to take the fun out of life for any of their clients. A challenge of this kind really ought to be thoughtfully and properly met.

I note and approve the aim of the Association as being more interested in the future than in the past, but I wonder if it is realistic. The past is secure, the present only reasonably so, and the future, even looking ahead to next Thanksgiving or Christmas is — who knows?

Perhaps, too, others will agree with me that it is unsporting of the Association to admit members as youthful as fifty-five. Why shouldn't they earn their way as we have done? Let them wait until they ripen on the vine.

Or does the Association really hedge on its interest in the future and turn away from real age to candidates with a better prospect?

❧

I wouldn't call Graham a long-range planner, but he shows some of the characteristics. When he gets to the corner of Sheriff's Lane and Pease's Point Way he invariably knows in which direction he wants to go. How does he know this? As for myself, I have seldom thought of the matter and can only assume that Graham has some fairly important reason. Naturally I follow his lead. How long has he been decided between north and south, the choice of routes through Simpson's Lane or Pease's Point Way to Morse or Cottage? I can't tell, and I am tempted unscientifically to assume he has considered factors of wind and weather and how the scents are likely to be in this direction or that. I do know that he remembers accurately where pleasant discoveries have been made, and that he likes to check on many of the same things from day to day. There is always some precinct or ward or commonwealth he has made his own, in which he tallies up the best and newest smells, taking note of trespassers. All this requires his attention and is part of his life, I think the only part, separable from mine. Neither of us likes to languish around. We have little patience with people and dogs who don't know their own minds.

Yesterday afternoon he chose Cottage Street, and at the corner of North Water we met two girls on bicycles, both wearing shorts and brightly colored shirts. They were out of season, obviously arrivals from afar, a new border state probably, close to the territory of sophistication. The younger one, not much past the age of twenty, I would think, though I am no longer qualified to judge, leaped from her bicycle exclaiming, "Oh, my collie is in Los Angeles!"

From California, then. I was right. I observed her slender cheeks, not yet filled out, and the narrowness of the eyes that gave her a piquant expression. She embraced Graham, to his delight, and ran her fingers through his ruff.

"He makes sounds just like my collie!" They mostly do, of course, though the expression varies a good deal.

"What's your collie's name?" I asked.

"Caprice."

It was a good name for a collie belonging to her. I thought she herself might well have had the same christening. Graham was now jumping up to deliver that gentle, generous lap of his tongue upon the cheek of Caprice's owner, and then jumping on me to share the joy of the moment. And so California the sophisticated met Graham and me of coastal Massachusetts, out of season, at the corner of Cottage and North Water. We parted in a mutual glow.

⌒

While summer was still with us, Graham and I went for a walk in the evening, and somehow one of the fireflies of the darkness along the path around Sheriff's Meadow Pond became positioned in Graham's ruff. "Somehow" is a word of explanation or more rightly of nonexplanation for things that nature, not even contriving, allows to happen all by themselves. Nature is easygoing and often at her best in a starlit and firefly-lit summer night at Sheriff's Meadow.

Along marched Graham, the firefly flashing on and off in his ruff, and the effect was as good as that of a candlelight processional or a watch night service. I thought, why does man exert himself so mightily instead of profiting by the example of nature, which — or who — stands gently by, when permitted, and follows a different impulse and livelier rulebook that says remarkable things will surely be revealed, maybe tonight, maybe tomorrow night, but at all events within the span of cosmic time?

A collie, full-coated and magnificently ruffed, and a firefly to flash on and off — these two on a warm-cool evening following a path through bayberry thickets, beside arrow-wood, wild cherry, dogwood, and the rest; what could be simpler, yet how worth collecting and storing in memory. Once having happened, though the like of it might not happen for many a summer, and though a small thing at best, it belonged in world experience and could never be expunged or taken away.

Eventually the firefly departed from Graham's ruff and blinked away through the night, and Graham was neither more nor less proud, or at all wiser, for the passenger he had carried and the show they both had made.

⌒

This summer retrospect was in my mind when I read about a 444-acre property in North Falmouth on the other side of Vineyard Sound, situated at the intersection of Sam Turner Road and Route 28, which I took to be a confrontation of easygoing old and enterprising new. I have no idea who Sam Turner may have been, but the genealogy of Route 28 and all such routes is familiar. This land had been projected for a residential development with a lot of "units."

But the Falmouth planning board had suggested that the owners consider, instead, "some proper kind of tourist attraction" — a "sophisticated Sturbridge Village" or something on the order of "Strawbery Banke" at Portsmouth,

New Hampshire, something "the town could be proud of."
Cape Cod, the board said, had become so built-up that it
suffered a lack of tourist attractions.

Since it is an unwritten but undisputed law that tourists
must be attracted, when one bait, or all old baits, are used
up, another must be found. The notion is in itself ironic,
but for relish of the situation one must go back to nature.
Once upon a time, the Cape, like Martha's Vineyard, lay
open and native under the sun, wonderful in its hills,
woods, and shore as Thoreau experienced them. But the
modern highway had brought Cape Cod within a day's
drive of the eastern megalopolis, tourists came, development invaded the bare and bended arm of Massachusetts.
Enterprise flourished. Its new name became Tourism. And
the original wonder was lost.

Now, simplicity long outgrown and overdressed, a 444-
acre tract at the intersection of Sam Turner Road and Route
28 offers an opportunity to contrive an imitation that will
look like the lost original, in a merchantable package with
built-in tourist appeal. Today's entrepreneurs can imitate
anything, even an old civilization, though not very well,
for coyness and artifice take the place of inner reality.

I say I am marked by the past so deeply that I lack
tolerance for such imitations, as some digestions are un-
equal to salt-water taffy; but I am also old and cranky.
Which is the greater truth makes no difference. A hired
hand from the drugstore corner, dressed in rusty coat and
beaver hat, both fireproofed and chemically aged, may belong on Route 28 but certainly not on Sam Turner Road.

Once again, what an odd thing time is. When it has long
enough gone by, there's still money to be made out of it.

∽

At the lighthouse yesterday morning we met a dog
named Bigelow. His coat was long-trailing and of a bluish

cast, and he had a ragged attractiveness. Raffish might be the word. His owner said he was very young, and he must have been, for he and Graham were happily met.

Meetings. Encounters. We enjoy them in the early morning. It is always good, for instance, to see Betty Holding with her dogs, Ginger and the pretentious little black one, nameless to me, who thinks he could lick Graham and would enjoy doing so, and her three cats. Only three? I think so, but I'm not sure, because they are strung out in an erratic, diversionary line, attending to things that cats like to attend to. There is something about it that might lead one to say, "There go all of us."

This morning the *Lindblad Explorer* came in, that cruise ship of which the likeness is seen in magazine advertisements so often that she symbolizes far seas and ports of the world. She belongs to Asia, Africa, and now Edgartown, though only by the way. The *Explorer* is by all odds the biggest vessel to make port here in the early morning or at any other time of day within the memory of living man. I mean my own memory, but it's all the same thing. Generations have passed since big ships entered the harbor at Edgartown.

We saw her first far out beyond Cape Pogue, and she came on, steadily larger and larger, as the earth turned slowly toward the sun beyond Chappaquiddick, the sky lighting and coloring, minute by minute, and the horizon left behind. We stood watching as she loomed and slackened speed abreast of the Harbor View, not a handsome vessel but a fascinating visitor all the same, her adventuring character plain to see. We heard voices on board and then at last the rattle of her anchor chain running out.

That was a sound to unite the ages — Nineveh, Tyneside, Table Bay, and all the rest. It was good to hear, especially in the fresh clear morning, and I thought of Masefield and

Conrad and — how many others? One brief sound in the morning, heard before and long ago, thrillingly remembered. The *Explorer* was against the red sunrise when the chain rattled out and the anchor dropped.

Edith Blake wrote later in the *Gazette* that the natives went out in small boats to go aboard, and the passengers came ashore to see the sights and trade for trinkets.

I T'S BEEN SUNNY and warm lately, and I've hung my wash out in the front yard where the elms are gone and the new sunlight is, never mind convention. Where were washed clothes hung out before drying yards were invented? And whoever heard of drying yards in the country? The suburbs, yes, of course. Some may say Graham and I live neither in the country nor the suburbs. That's a question, the way things go nowadays, but small towns do survive, even if barely.

It is true that we live within five blocks of the post office, but Betty and I built where the town runs off, not into slumlike disarray, but into the region named a hundred and fifty years ago Sheriff's Meadow. There's no real meadow, or ever was, for a few rods from our door wildness takes over. At its heart is Sheriff's Meadow Pond, anciently an ice pond which required integrity lest the ice be tainted.

A different integrity has taken over now, in the name of
ecology, and at home in the pond or over it are great blue
herons, kingfishers, snowy egrets, yellow warblers, snap-
ping turtles, an otter family. We meet, though not too
closely, Graham and I, and they, in the whole round of the
year.

If it were not for a dike built by devoted ancestors of the
hamlet there would be a slough, not a pond. Sheriff's
Meadow is, in brief, a "made" pond. Louis H. Pease used
to let the waters out once a year for a few weeks to prepare
the way for new rains and clear ice. This was when the
great gray icehouse stood beside the pond, a landmark
shouldering high above the landscape, though not too high
in the view from our house. Weathering makes for con-
tentment in buildings, and the icehouse was weathered and
gently sagging. A feeling of quietude and husbandry continues now, though the pond banks are grown up with wild
cherry, viburnum, poison ivy, woodbine, tall-bush blueberry — all the native trees and thickets — and the dogwood, red maple, holly, and tulip trees I planted when I
was much younger than I am now.

People speak of "the tunnel," the completely shaded
path one follows to come out presently in the surprising
openness of the dike and its world view — the white tower
of the Methodist Church and town clock against the sky
and closely reflected in the waters of the pond by sunlight,
starlight, or moonglow; a short overflow creek running into
John Butler's Mud Hole, so called in ancient deeds; and a
longer creek from the Mud Hole to the Eel Pond and Nantucket Sound, with remote Cape Cod (the enemy mainland) for a backdrop. Cape Cod mutters with detonations
as planes break the sound barrier above Otis Field.

All this and a good deal more, native grown both in wildness and civility, upon which Graham and I look out as we

keep our appointments by day or night. The house still pretends that it faces Pierce Lane and the life of the town, as it does in a way. But even along Pierce Lane wild apple trees grow and bloom beside our weathered and mossy board fence.

I hung my undershirts and shorts on a line crosswise of the front yard where they made a modest showing, I thought, though on the other hand perhaps they were uncomfortably private. My shirts swayed on their hangers in shades of blue, yellow, green, and one Christmas shirt of striped blue, lavender, and white. They offered a salute to me, if to no one else, as if they represented my coat of arms, unburdened by any lineage except that of the day and hour. For a better effect I can buy some gay towels advertised in the magazines.

Meantime, how quickly clothes dry in the sunshine and open air, and how fine the reliance upon free energy. Milton Birch is quite right, though the season now is wrong for wild roses. All I have noticed so far is the satisfying dry cleanliness of October's exulting northwest wind.

⌁

There was a party late Sunday afternoon at Edie Blake's mother's boathouse on the Edgartown harbor front for Hiram Haydn's account of his career in publishing, *Words & Faces* — what a good title! Hiram wasn't among the company of his friends and fellow-Islanders, for he died tragically last December. Should one, after all, say "tragically," since death is an appointed part of life, even though the end of life as well? Perhaps not, strictly, but in the context of achievement, happy and promising outlook, friendship, and humanity, yes.

The party in honor of Hiram and the book was marvelously warm-spirited, with Mary as hostess, Michael and

Miranda beside her, and so many friends who were of high accomplishment themselves, or had been helped in the profession of words by Hiram's wisdom and shared experience, or were perhaps close simply in Island ties and outlook. Stan Hart of the Red Cat bookstore in North Tisbury stood ready with copies of *Words & Faces*, not to be autographed with pen and ink but in the lonely imagined writing of the heart.

So many said, aloud or to themselves, "Too bad Hiram is not here." He was there, of course, in the memory of his friends, and this as good a reality as almost any other.

When I got home I read over again a great deal of what he had put down about his active life in writing, editing, and publishing that ended when he was still sixty-six. So much too young. I came across a passage about Irwin Edman he had reprinted from *The American Scholar*. "When a true voice is stilled, one little relishes chirping in its place, even in tribute."

Then he quoted from one of Edman's *American Scholar* columns: "Nor, as a matter of fact, with respect to either personal or public events, does one often remotely know that this is the end. One leaves a friend in perfect health and the next day hears he is dead."

Nor did the friend know, either, I think. In his "De Senectute," Cicero wrote, "No one is so old that he does not expect to live a year longer." I, at seventy-eight, certainly have that much expectation. More, even.

Further in this column quoted by Hiram, Edman introduced lines from Edna St. Vincent Millay's address to Persephone about a friend who had just died:

> Say to her, "My dear, my dear,
> It is not so dreadful here."

Then one of Edman's own affirmations: "Serenity can come only from seeing events in that light of eternity which is commonly called philosophy"; and another: "I have good authority for believing that in larger matters it is simply world without end."

No wonder, then, that in the warm but soberly thoughtful frame of mind in which I had come from the party, I turned to other passages written by Irwin Edman, whom I also knew, though peripherally, from college days through intervals of chance renewal. His philosophy of naturalism even I could understand.

"It is not my purpose here to raise all the age-old controversy as to whether God exists or whether His beneficent purposes are attested by nature. I wish to point out simply that a sense of meaning, of value, of purpose can be found in existence without recourse to any world beyond that which scientific knowledge reveals."

That is from *Religion Without Tears* and so is this:

"The sadness that comes from recognition that individual life ends with the grave is mitigated for any generous mind by the continuity of the adventure of mankind, and the participation, even briefly, in the shape of things to come."

I tasted these words carefully, especially the phrase "even if briefly." Cicero wrote, "To me no life seems long that has any end." The longer the better, I say, but the generous mind should not boggle at whatever the measure promises or threatens to be.

Most of my contemporaries, those of us who are eligible for membership in the Association of Retired Persons, including the relatively junior and also some too infirm to go to meetings, are readier to embrace comforting promises of conventional religion than to take up the lantern of philosophy. After threescore years and ten they find skepticism debilitating, and after eighty they are easily confirmed in reassuring faith.

Cicero had the same inclination. He wrote "De Senectute" at the age of sixty-three but put his words in the mouth of such older men as Marcus Portius Cato Censorious, who learned Greek in his advanced years. One translator says that old age is portrayed by Cicero "as it may be, not as it generally is."

Anyway, Cicero has Cato saying, "Yet I depart from life as from an inn, not as from a home; for nature has given us here a lodging for a sojourn, not a place of habitation. O glorious day, when I shall go to that divine company and assembly of souls, and when I shall depart from this crowd and tumult!" "De Senectute" might have been written in this part by any of our modern clerics who specialize in best-selling books of comfort.

"When the constitution of man is dissolved by death," Cicero quotes Cato, "it is obvious what becomes of each of the other parts; for they all go whence they came: but the soul alone is invisible, alike when it is present and when it departs."

Irwin Edman simplifies this problem, comparing the soul or spirit to the flame of the candle.

I turn to the letter Huxley wrote to Kingsley: "But the longer I live, the more obvious it is to me that the most sacred act of a man's life is to say and to feel, 'I believe such and such to be true.' All the greatest rewards and all the heaviest penalties of existence cling about that act. The universe is one and the same throughout; and if the condition of my success in unravelling some little difficulty of anatomy or physiology is that I shall rigorously refuse to put faith in that which does not rest on sufficient evidence, I cannot believe that the great mysteries of existence will be laid open to me on other terms."

This impassioned, astringent realism appeals to me as much at seventy-eight as it did at fifty-eight when I first read it.

But there is much in Cicero that I like, including this catalogue of old men. Who would not be glad to make his way into such a list!

". . . Plato, who died while writing in his eighty-first year . . . Isocrates, who says that he wrote the book called 'Panathenicus' in his ninety-fourth year and lived years afterward . . . Leontinus Gorgias filled out one hundred and seven years without suspending his study and his labor. When he was asked why he was willing to live so long, he replied, 'I have no fault to find with old age.' "

The light of eternity — I have no idea what it is or how to seek it. I can only proceed with my daily assignments, beginning with the morning walk to the lighthouse, the glow of which guards one nocturnal round at a time.

Graham and I were up at five this morning, when the stars guided us as surely as if we had been mariners at sea, although we knew the way well enough and did not get into any primitive country until we entered Bob Brown's moor. The air had cleared from yesterday's rain, the wind gusted heartily from the northwest, and I was pleased to have put on an extra sweater. We saw no one until we reached Main Street on the way to the office where the *Vineyard Gazette* will be printed today, for this is another Friday. There we crossed courses with Henry Delaney, who was bound on some early errand, and exchanged our first good mornings across the street.

No other sign of dawn but Orion paling in the northern sky. Orion had seen something that as yet we hadn't, and wouldn't for an hour longer.

 ⌣

Our domestic arrangements. My sister-in-law expressed more than ordinary surprise when I happened to mention "Graham's room."

"What did you say?" she asked.

"Graham's room," I repeated.

I will explain the circumstances. My house, as it is now, though I still think of it as Betty's and mine, has seven rooms. Back in 1928 when it was built, everybody called it a big house. This was mostly because it rose well above the highest ground on the lot, with good distances around it. A house in the middle of an open field, asserting itself a little, looks like a big house no matter what. White paint, green shutters, and a calculated sense of Edgartown tradition also contributed to the effect.

On the first floor is a central hall which is a place for people to come in, a staircase to rise out of, and so on. Houses nowadays are likely to have "areas" instead of rooms. To me the word that goes most naturally with "areas" is "disputed," and I am glad of the old plan. The central hall is also a horizontal shaft of air and light. It affords a long view. One may easily stand under the ancient mulberry tree at our front gate in the old board fence along Pierce Lane and see across the lawn, through the house, and as far on the other side as the tangle of vines on Sheriff's Lane. I have never measured this distance because what it seems to be is so much more than feet or yards could show.

A central hall requires more heating but its interrupting channel encourages thought and detachment. Standing there after a minute or two you feel you aren't anywhere, and can even forget in which direction you were headed. To be on the way somewhere, surrounded by house, and maybe a creaking sound high above in the attic, is to hold time momentarily in your hand. The hall is also useful for turning around in and for piling hats and coats on a bench inside the front door.

The living room is on the left as one enters. Everyone

needs a living room, or thinks so. We called ours a "sitting room" when I was a boy in New Bedford, and we had a parlor too. Time has passed. But where now could I sit before a fire on the hearth except in a living room? In an "area" I suppose, but one would have to become long accustomed to it.

Keeping books is one of the room's best uses. On the shelves that cover all the space of the west wall are more than I have read or ever will, but their company is congenial, and I look into them for many good reasons. There's a bar in my living room, and everyone knows how essential that is.

Across the hall is the dining room which Graham and I use principally for walking through to get to the kitchen. But last night I did serve a chicken chowder there for my neighbors, Catherine Woodrow and Edith Blake, and the room warmed cheerily for the first time in almost a year. Chicken chowder is a convenient main course, for it spends most of its time on the stove, is patient to the moment of dishing up, and makes its own way on the table. There's nothing finicky about it, and if there is any left over it improves with age. One should plan to have some left, if possible, but the plan is likely to fail.

My kitchen is the home of the usual facilities — stove, sink, washing machine, dishwasher, and "fridge," as the term now is. The equipment I knew as a boy was different: a coal-burning range, an icebox in a back storeroom, kept supplied by an iceman, and a soapstone sink which my mother would still prefer to stainless steel. She could be right. The dishwasher I don't use too often, but it is a timesaver to have on hand. Instead of twenty minutes or half an hour of delay on dishwashing days, Graham and I can be off in an old-fashioned trice for our morning walk.

The washing machine "does" the clothes that I hang out

in the front yard in the sunlight, and it has a flat top on which I dump the mail and odds and ends when I arrive home from the *Gazette*, the market, or the post office. The miscellany quickly turns to litter. I don't defend that except to say that litter has the advantage of ease and relaxation. The routing of my important papers is usually from kitchen to dining room to living room, then upstairs, then down again, and a division of residue between rubbish cans in Sheriff's Lane and outgoing mail. It's a close thing as to which. But sometimes things get filed, and sometimes I can find them later on.

In the kitchen is the table by the windows where I sit at meals, looking out at my birds feeding under the wild cherry trees or on the rosa multiflora bush. Things ramble out there — bittersweet, turquoise berry, everything fruitful and viny. Long ago I planted a mulberry tree that came in a special offer of seedling trees at ten cents each. I lost track of most of them, but the mulberry really took hold and now has a big trunk and branches reaching way up above the kitchen wing of the house, from which it showers the ground with insipid purple fruit in summer. The birds enjoy it, but only mildly, not by first choice.

My birds, as I call them, appear in shifts throughout the year. I now have my twenty or so white-throated sparrows which check in the last of each September and stay until time to fly north in gayer plumage when their springtime comes. I saw two robins and a catbird yesterday, but they should be on their way south. They rate as summer people, but there will be robins from farther north arriving to winter in our swamps, and I shall glimpse some of them occasionally. Redwings always hang on late, and so do grackles. Cardinals, blue jays, song sparrows, myrtle warblers, chickadees, and starlings I have with me all year. And there will always be the visitors of opportunity at chosen times and seasons.

I am old enough to have outlived three electric refrigerators — or is it four? But my father at eighty-seven was outlived by his icebox, though at the latter end he couldn't get ice for it and used it for keeping string, bottle caps, tacks, and clothespins.

The kitchen represents and sometimes caricatures my way of life. It combines work-saving, extravagance, and very little thrift. It also represents arrival and departure, for Graham and I are usually going somewhere or just coming in, and the kitchen door is the convenient one. Our eating time is short.

Now I will go upstairs for the important letter I must not forget to mail. It's probably in the pocket of my coat over a chairback in the kitchen, but I don't know that yet.

Upstairs there were originally four bedrooms, now reconsidered. The smallest has become my study. It's an easygoing room with typewriter, books, used and unused paper, litter everywhere, especially on the floor, and provision for keeping things and for losing things. I am whelmed in deeper gulfs than most. I can reflect, though the reflection neither hinders nor helps, that in this room I have written or assembled the twenty-one books that bear my name on the covers. This speaks of continuity but not of stability; only one of those books stayed around very long.

The view from the north windows behind my chair has changed little through the years. Even when I do not turn my head I am aware of the ancient ice pond of Sheriff's Meadow and blue Nantucket Sound beyond. But I do look out, watching the change of days, so many signs along the journey I make with the earth around the sun.

For a very long time I slept in a four-poster in the southwest bedroom. The point of a broken spring worked up through the mattress but I avoided it without much trouble and did not put myself to the expense of change. The abating of a nuisance can be worse than the nuisance itself. One wants the privilege of leaving oneself alone. Then for the years of Betty's illness I moved into the blue bedroom on the blustery northeast side of the house. I became accustomed to the severer climate and found enough margin on the single bed for Graham when he arrived.

But Graham grew rapidly until in bed at night I found myself too much the lesser partner. Graham settled in to suit himself and refused to budge. So I moved back to the four-poster, and on the first night of my return was punctured by the point of the broken spring. What had been easy before was impossible now. As for Graham, he wouldn't even try the four-poster because he considered it too high above the floor.

I went to Vineyard Haven and bought a new three-quarter size bed which I intended for Graham and myself. But when the new bed had been set up, the four-poster relegated to the cellar, Graham was not interested. He turned on his heels and went back to the single bed in his own room. What else should it be called?

I have accounted for three bedrooms, including the one that became my study. The fourth, on the southeast corner, is the master bedroom, unslept in now for almost ten years. It rejoices in the best sunlight of winter and summer alike, it is neat and proper, and it has a Christmas cactus in one window and an inconveniently located telephone on a bedside table. I have not bothered to have the telephone changed. When it rings I rush to it from my study on the gallop and usually am on time, sometimes to my regret.

Of course this master bedroom was where Betty and I slept long ago, but I do not preserve its idle and neat condition for the sake of memory. Memory is everywhere, not to be partitioned off, and I find the best of it outdoors.

Such are our domestic arrangements, Graham's and mine. Have I no feeling of guilt at occupying this seven-room house with Graham, when so many human beings, companions of a difficult world, must do without a decent place to sleep? Not really, for time's statute of limitations will set in soon enough. Our tenancy is for today and so few other days, used up quickly, one by one. I think that we represent the last of a civilization of the possible, and the new civilization, if it is that, may well be of the impossible. What that means, I can hardly guess.

This chapter of my house is also my chapter of Time Passes, illuminated by old stars and possibly new ones, astir always with low sounds, and patterned with changing cloud, sunlight, and moonlight.

This morning Graham and I stood at the end of the causeway as the sun appeared directly opposite the lighthouse, its rays divided on either side. The appointment was one we had been waiting for, and it was a satisfaction to have things work out so exactly. After this the sun will appear a little at the south of the lighthouse.

∽

Yesterday I took one of those half-size stepladders from the kitchen into the living room and began rearranging books on the top shelves. They had not been disturbed for many years. Most of them were little books, and two or three came tumbling down. Nearest to my feet was *The Prisoner of Zenda*, and this surprised me because I did not know there was a copy in the house. Betty must have brought it from her home in Pennsylvania.

I looked at the title page: "Henry Holt and Company, 1894" — two years before I was born. But in my boyhood at Fish Hook, our old Vineyard house way off in the country beyond the end of the Indian Hill Road, I played the game of Authors in the evenings around the living room table and the kerosene lamp with the white shade. It was a Juno lamp. Anthony Hope was one of the authors and *The Prisoner of Zenda* one of the books. I tried now to think of some of the others and managed a few: Gilbert Parker and *The Seats of the Mighty*, Hall Caine and *The Manxman*, also *The Eternal City*, and Anthony Hope's *The Dolly Dialogues*.

I left off with my rearranging and sat down for a while with *The Prisoner of Zenda*:

> "Your ring will always be on my finger, your heart in my heart, the touch of your lips on mine. But you must go and I must stay . . ."
>
> There struck on our ears the sound of singing. The priests in the chapel were singing masses for the souls of those who lay dead. They seemed to chant a requiem over our buried joy, to pray forgiveness for our love that would not die. The soft, sweet, pitiful music rose and fell as we stood opposite one another, her hands in mine.
>
> "My queen and my beauty," I said.
>
> "My lover and true knight," she said. "Perhaps we shall never see one another again. Kiss me, my dear, and go!"
>
> I kissed her as she bade me; but at the last she clung to me, whispering nothing but my name, and that over and over again — and again — and again; and then I left her.

I can't say that I was or was not moved by this scene of renunciation, for I was so deeply moved by memory of a time when this was seriously read, my own time, really, that it all came to the same thing. I am still not grown from my own childhood, which is quite a different thing from saying that I am not grown up. I will not let go my birthright.

The sad parting of Rudolf Rassendyll and Princess Flavia was still in my mind when I happened across another scene of renunciation in a brand new book I had just bought at Stanley Hart's shop — *The Ebony Tower* by John Fowles, published eighty years after *The Prisoner of Zenda*.

There had been an embrace in the moonlight.

He had meant it to be very brief. But once he found her mouth and felt her body, her arms around him, it had no hope of being brief . . . and again inside the house he felt the quick press of her mouth against his. Then she was walking toward the stairs . . .

"Just let me hold you for a little."

"It would only make it worse."

"But if an hour ago you . . ."

"That was someone else. And I was someone else."

"Perhaps they were right."

She looked down the corridor at her own door.

"Where will you be this time tomorrow, David?"

"I still want to go to bed with you."

"Out of charity?"

"Wanting you."

"Fuck and forget?"

Well, there it goes. They parted. There was no pitiful music, soft and sweet, but he "whispered her name in a kind of incredulous despair" which was almost as good as whispering it over again and again — and again. Of the two passages I prefer the earlier, for from Zenda to Coetminais is a long journey for me to take.

We would have outgrown the old in any case without the gulf opened by Freud, and it did not need to be shamed, so that we must atone and, as if by way of penitence, adopt the obscene (as I still think of it) as the natural way of speech.

How long I have lived, and how strong the temptation would be to go back if I could. How wide is the separation in books as in so much else between my boyhood and shadowed age. I think I know of much that has been lost while I looked on. The new age must hold to its poses with new attitudes every year but hardly more enlightenment and integrity than the time of my youth held to its conventions. We are better off in knowledge today but I am not sure we are better off in the use we make of it.

Although I played the game of Authors by lamplight at
Fish Hook in the first decade of this century, impressed by
the names of books I took to be classics, my acquaintance
with *The Prisoner of Zenda* was never close. I did not read
the book, though sometime in the early 1920s I saw the
motion picture in New York in the company of Bill Roberts,
and not an hour later recognized one of the film actors
walking up Broadway.

"Look!" I exclaimed to Bill. "There's Rupert of Hent-
zau!" I spoke more loudly than I intended, and Rupert
heard me and stared at us with a disagreeable expression.
In his street attire he looked more like a Damon Runyon
character than one contrived by Sir Anthony Hope
Hawkins for the court of Ruritania.

In literature as in wine there is a pre-Phylloxera vintage,
and what made the difference was Freud. There is no going back, and now we have to rely upon Freud as we do
upon electricity or penicillin.

In the kitchen just now I thought I heard someone moving outside, but it was only the leaves falling.

I have at last accounted for the fact that the number of
socks I take out of the washing machine is almost always
uneven, so that I cannot make them up in pairs. Either I
didn't put enough into the machine in the first place or
failed to allow for the one I dropped on the way to the
kitchen.

Graham doesn't altogether take me seriously, and I don't
know why I bother to say "altogether."

There are depressed times, as when one feels an important appointment has been forever lost. Sara Teasdale

put this best in her poem "The Long Hill." All the morning she thought how proud she would be "to stand there
straight as a queen,/Wrapped in the wind and the sun with
the world under me." But "it was nearly level along the
beaten track" and "the rest of the way will be only going
down." One wonders what the view might have been if,
fully aware, one had stopped to look.

The best treatment for depression in my own case is to
wait it out. But I do value the counsel of the friendly
psychiatrist I quoted a while back.

> I would wonder if what you are calling depression has
> some relationship to considerable criticism of yourself for
> the way you have treated yourself in the course of a life-
> time, principally for the things you have not done just for
> the pleasure and satisfaction of them and of yourself. One
> can get quite bitter about this. Sometimes it helps to be
> philosophical and to recall that at the time we developed
> inhibitions and enforced them, we did so to avoid what
> might have been unendurable anxiety; and, indeed, our
> defenses have worked so well that we have at least gotten
> old without any major disaster.

The backward look is not limited to nostalgia, guilt, or
repentance. Here, even, is Freud offering mitigation and
reassurance, if we can learn gently to sort things out.
There's an internal realism, slow in coming and requiring
help, a soberer self-appraisal than was possible in earlier
years. What have we lived for if not to see ourselves more
clearly with the same improvement in view that we can
enjoy in regard to other prospects? Those inhibitions and
defenses, hidden at the time — otherwise they couldn't have
existed at all — ought now to be sufficiently isolated for us
to identify and examine them with detachment.

My depressions usually lift as the sun rises, though not
always. Sometimes I am dogged by the errors and embar-

rassments of my past life. There are so many of them. How could I have been so raw and foolish? So wasteful? So inconsiderate? I suffer in what might be called my soul.

A balanced relationship with the past is so impossible to maintain that one must go on precariously with both old and new pitfalls threatening, one as real, though maybe deceptively, as the other. Balancing is not what I do best at my time of life, though I think I tend to improve.

Some old people can see the horizon all around, and almost always clearly. Our friend Dr. Walton Brooks McDaniel is one of these at the age of 104. He has long prevented anyone else from enjoying the pleasure of being the oldest graduate of Harvard. He likes to recall how he threatened to flunk Franklin D. Roosevelt in a Harvard Latin course, with salutary results, and he can still push a wheelbarrow.

Perspective is long in coming, but there are helps of a simple and natural kind. A walk in the woods is often useful, the more miles the better. The clarity and sweetness of the air are healing, and the drifting, falling leaves help to cover over the way one has traveled.

∽

I have found a crumpled memorandum in my jacket pocket, evidently not an old one, though I cannot recall its occasion: "Red Label Bourbon, Gin, Vodka, Tonic water, Bitter Lemon, Wine." Maybe I am living a gayer old age than I had been aware.

∽

When I began keeping house for Graham and myself, with his help of course — neither of us could do it alone — I was determined that everything should be neat and ship-shape. As a model, I recalled my mother's kitchen in New

Bedford long ago, and its cleanliness that came from one principle and practice, scrubbing. Kitchens had a lot of wood in my mother's day: floors, dressers as we called them (they are more often referred to as "counters" nowadays), and shelves in pantry and closets. There were no synthetic table tops or steel cabinets or fancy floors. Scrubbed wood looked clean and smelled clean. I'm not surprised that scrubbing has become so nearly obsolete, though. It took a lot of muscle and time.

My kitchen is so modern that wiping, shining, polishing, rinsing, and the rest have taken the place of scrubbing. So my purpose of neatness ought to have been served easily. The requirements were simple: to keep things picked up, no soiled dishes or fragments of lettuce and whatnot left in the sink, no crumbs in the corners or behind the toaster, no traces of egg on the table, no litter.

At first I planned to do some cooking of a plain variety. Once I made a lamb stew that lasted five days. It improved as it went along, but I didn't plan on another for quite a while. Now a couple of years have passed, and I will have to look up the recipe again. I saved labor and favored my own taste by leaving out carrots and turnips.

But all my cooking has fallen off until it is reserved for special occasions. Why go to so much trouble just for Graham and myself? Opening cans and packages is much simpler, and a lot of things you can eat raw as the Eskimos do.

The discipline of maintaining an immaculate kitchen began to seem out of proportion to the profit thereof, for who besides myself was likely to know the condition of my sink or floor or stove? Lillian came two days a week, but I always straightened things up before she arrived for real cleaning and tidying. Anyway, I knew she would be supportive.

So gradually I relaxed my management practices with a sense of peace and security. I became inured to the sight of soiled plates in the sink, crumbs and mud on the floor, eggshells in fragments here and there, and an atmosphere of someone having eaten a meal, or two or three, and each time having gone out in a hurry.

Hurry can be the best part of leisure if you know how. You do it when you don't have to, when there is no compulsion at all, and the gain is all in your state of mind or body. Hurry is escape when escape is not a necessity but an indulgence.

But am I exposing a fault of character? At least I hang up my pajamas every morning, and open my bed to the air. I think my bringing up was pretty good, yet the wear and tear of time and circumstance can make all sorts of difference. I waive all this and stand on the conclusive advantage of age. There are worse eccentricities than leaving tea leaves, melon rinds, mouldy bread, and dishes that smell of sour milk at large in the kitchen. I am putting the worst face on the matter, and claim that I am beyond any occasion when it would have been worthwhile for me to enforce the habits of my youth.

I went in at the beginning of something or other and have come out at the far end. Nobody is trained as my mother trained me.

My breakfast is of fruit or fruit juice, three or four Shredded Wheat biscuits with milk and maybe a little honey instead of sugar, and one or two cups of coffee, depending. Then I am out for that early morning walk, which usually doesn't take more than three quarters of an hour, even with lingering at the lighthouse.

I like to be at home by seven and at the typewriter, writing either for the *Vineyard Gazette* or for myself. Work is something to hang on to, and one likes to feel the shape and size of it, and to get the better of it while opportunity lasts. Everything about this arrangement is agreeable to Graham.

Hobbies are advocated for the old and are commendable, but for most of us I think they turn out to be fluctuating and unreliable. The bench and tools in the cellar are likely to be neglected after a while, additions to the bird list come slowly, and it's tiresome to have to milk the goat in the back yard.

Temperament figures a good deal in the choice of hobbies, and some elderly men and women attack them successfully. I am acquainted with a Mrs. Wilbraham who was once a worldly person, or at least an international one, and is a collector of hobbies. The collecting itself being the hobby, she cannot lose. She invited me to tea the other day.

She is a sprightly person behind rather prim nineteenth-century features that disguise the volatile inwardness of her temperament. Her house is a small one hidden by pine trees at the western rim of town. There's no view of the harbor for her, but the pines stir and murmur with the sound of sea waves.

"I'm not offering you any gin," Mrs. Wilbraham said, the moment we were seated. "Because I don't believe in cutting down all those juniper trees."

I said that it was only the juniper berries that were used, that no harm comes to the trees, and anyway she had asked me for tea.

"I'm going to put a little rum in mine," she said. "That was just a manner of speaking. I don't care for gin."

After the usual fussing, she poured the tea. I declined the suggestion of rum.

"An older person gets to be a toper," she said, "though with me it's just a habit of trying things. If you don't try them, how do you know what they are? I see that the adult education classes are starting up again at the schoolhouse. Who's going to teach creative writing this year?"

"I don't know."

"Weren't you asked?"

"Not this year."

"Well, I may take the course anyway. I don't know. I don't suppose it makes any real difference who the instructor is. I've taken so many Great Books courses that it would be a change-off if I try the writing end. So far as the creative part goes, I'm all right. Wouldn't you think that's more than half?"

I wasn't prepared to say. I retreated into the observation that creative writing would be worthwhile for its own sake and if she thought well of the course she would make no mistake in enrolling for it. On second thought I refrained from telling her about a young man of my acquaintance who, after World War II, hesitated between using his G.I. benefits for learning to write short stories or instruction in how to raise mink.

Mrs. Wilbraham did decide to enroll and went to several classes before choosing to raise gloxinias instead. Not everyone can be a switch hobbyist like her.

∽

Graham and I have so few differences that I am surprised lately at his determination to change the course of our morning walk. He is affable about the matter but in his quiet way firm, not to say stubborn. My goal remains the Harbor Light and if possible the predawn eastern sky. There's nothing extraordinary about the light itself. It's just a sturdy and graceful white cone as so many old lighthouses are. The lighthouse service brought it down from Ipswich some years ago when we no longer needed a keeper, and what had been the keeper's house was torn down.

For several mornings Graham lingered in the lane beside our back gate, letting me know he didn't like the direction I was taking.

"Off to the lighthouse!" I said to him. He refused to hear.

He waited, watching closely, until I reached the mouth of the lane. I turned right instead of left, and the diversion attracted him as I had meant it to do. He came loping after me, and we doubled back and walked to the lighthouse.

The next day he waited again, making it clear that he wished to walk around the pond, no argument about it. I tried another stratagem by starting around the pond and cutting off sharply through the hedgerow gap and then past the tennis courts to resume our usual course to the lighthouse. I don't think Graham was long deceived, but he accompanied me with good heart, and we headed across Bob Brown's moor with its ruddy grass and fading wild asters, along with the remembering loneliness of a summer lost. So this time we approached the lighthouse from the north instead of from the south, glimpsing the new sun first from the height of Starbuck's Neck.

One morning more, and this improvisation was used up. Graham watched me pass the tennis courts, allowed me to proceed from there, and himself returned to the lane and the back gate where I found him when I arrived home. He is as well aware as I that an early morning walk is for *us*, not for me alone, and he had delivered his ultimatum. First choice around the pond, or else. I hadn't experienced much vexation, but whatever it amounted to, was easily relaxed as I reflected that Graham was entitled to his own point of view, for whatever obscure reasons.

So this morning, bright with November crispness, the

sunlight barely touching the tops of the trees, chimneys, and ridges of the open country, Graham and I set out with common purpose to walk around the pond. Beyond the dike is the knoll where Graham ran swift circles in his lolloping, looping gallop, blond coat glistening, ruff and tail flung to the breeze, though I think the breeze was mostly of his own making. He charged past me narrowly two or three times, four feet in the air, until the surge of his energy was at last subdued. Then we continued through the twisting swamp path and home through the grove where the sugar maples are.

We stood again by the back gate, and I informed Graham that we were going to the lighthouse. As nearly as I can interpret his response, and I can hit it closely, he said, "Of course." So we did walk to the lighthouse, together and in complete rapport. I may refer to this as our first compromise — around the pond and then to the lighthouse.

It might be thought that Graham had triumphed, but what mattered to me was that early appointment with the eastern sky and the look of harbor and bay under the first new light, whether moody or glowing, tranquil or restive.

Emerson wrote:

> I am the owner of the sphere,
> Of the seven stars and the solar year . . .

This is flying pretty high, but if it was all right with Emerson it is all right with me.

At the end of the causeway I turned to look back at the town being freshly born again, coming alight before it was fully awake. Before such a glance familiarity turns into surprise. Have these houses always been so white, the sloping lawns so green, the wharf spiles standing in such rhythmic patterns? So, indeed, but never just so. Today is different, and its mode of arrival unexpected.

Now Graham and I have been home again for half an

hour or so. A mockingbird is singing November into another summer day, the sunlight clear, the earth not yet turned cold.

I have begun feeding the birds again. There are a lot of them on the ground a little way from the kitchen windows and under the wild cherry trees: bluejays, whitethroats back from the north, redwings staying late around the pond, mourning doves, a chewink or two, the exciting cardinals. My underwear, white and homely for the most part, hangs on the line along with two big bath towels and the brick red pants I wore yesterday.

∽

Lillian couldn't come, so this morning I have turned the mattress on my bed. I shirked the end-for-end procedure and simply wrestled the right side over to the left side so that what had been up and toward the windows became what is down and toward the wall. The dead weight of the mattress was nothing much, except that it did not stay dead. A mattress, though limp, is acrobatic by design. It twists and falls into contrary postures, and you can't tell where the center of gravity is or where it will be an instant from now. If there were a Beaufort scale for the tractability of mattresses, mine would be at the stormiest end of the range. Yet it is only a three-quarter size. I should stop talking about the mattress and talk instead about my age. It tells in all such household things.

When I was young I rejected the notion that mattresses had to be turned. So much housewifely nonsense, I thought, like washing windows whether they needed it or not. It wouldn't make any difference to a mattress if it just stayed put. But I am wiser now. The mattress does know the difference. Repeatedly I have found the matrix of my body confronting me at bedtime.

Having won the athletic exercise, I deferred the making

of the bed until later. Too much later, for I found it still unmade at eleven-thirty at night when my dinner guests had departed and I had accompanied Graham on a last star-lit rounding of the pond.

Just before midnight is not a preferred time for an amateur to make a bed. I recruited all my remaining skills after the long depletion of the day, executed a broken march back and forth around the bed, and finally had the sheets nearly enough in place though not neatly matched or tucked in. Then, carefully, I managed to effect a precarious entry between the covers. At least no part of me stuck out into the night chill. Whether the mattress was nubbly I did not notice, for I became lost in slumber more quickly and completely than usual.

Graham came into my room to see me at least once during the night. When he visits he usually brings something with him, and this time it was an undershirt retrieved from wherever I had dropped it.

～

To be both accurate and fair I must not make myself appear too healthy. I wouldn't want to be set apart from the companionship of my age and generation more than the facts justify, and even the facts are subject to change day by day. We all have our troubles. There's always arthritis, isn't there?

One morning last winter when I went downstairs, I leaned over to pull a night-light from its baseboard socket. To straighten up suddenly became so painful that I stopped trying. What, the old riddle asks, walks on four legs in the morning, two at noon, and three at night? As I walked to the kitchen, lacking a cane but showing a bent-over need for it, I remembered the riddle from my childhood and knew that for the time being, anyway, I had come to the final stage.

After a painfully constrained breakfast I set out into the wintry blackness with Graham, bent not quite so much as at first, but leaning a decisive bit from the perpendicular. I had abandoned the idea of going all the way to the lighthouse but I was determined to feed the ducks on Edie Blake's beach. We had established a regular tryst with the harbor ducks that bitter winter.

I felt, or thought I felt, like Old Gobbo, though if this was the case Shakespeare was cruel in opening Gobbo's infirmities to so much laughter. As soon as feasible I went to see Dr. Bob Nevin, to whom, of course, my difficulty was by no means unfamiliar. I don't recall that he put a name to it, but he gave me an injection of butazolidin which for twenty-four hours not only erased all discomfort but gave me the illusion of renewed youth. My spirit became jubilant and I was ready to go forth and conquer, though I don't remember what.

But the drug was only for shock treatment, and my euphoria soon died. I became Old Gobbo again overnight, with no laughter, much pain, and a figure bent far toward the double.

Physical therapy was now the thing, and I became a patient of Helen Erickson, a therapist of long experience and skill. My back, she informed me, was as hard and as rigid as a board. That was a good description of how it seemed to me, too. With massage and repeated exercises it gradually came back to the condition of being reasonably supple.

The exercise I liked best was "reaching for a star." I was glad to reach for a star, and pleased to have a medically approved gesture called by that phrase. Previously it had been advised only by teachers in the Parker Street School in New Bedford — "ad astra per aspera" was a reasonable approximation in my boyhood. I reached for many stars, caught none as expected (neither did Henry Thoreau), and soon friends and acquaintances were telling me how awful my appearance had been, and how shocked they had been to see me in such a condition. This was good to hear, more as a sign of recovery, since they were talking in the past tense, than because of the sympathy involved.

During my disability Helen wanted to see an X-ray of my back so that she could suit her ministrations more precisely to the trouble. Dr. Bob arranged an appointment for me at the Martha's Vineyard Hospital, where I was greeted at the desk and sent on to the proper department. Two young male technicians were in charge, and on their instruction I divested myself of most of my clothing and took up a pose on the X-ray table.

"The doctor is here and she'll look at it now," said the first technician when the X-ray had buzzed. We have long had plenty of women's lib on our Island, and Dr. Eliot, our roentgenologist, is a prime example.

I hadn't long to wait. Presently both the first and second technicians were back.

"We're going to take a couple more pictures," said Number One, and he and his companion rearranged me, retreated and took the pictures.

They went again. I waited, and back they came. More pictures. Dr. Eliot wanted to know how old I was. I did not hold back. A couple of times I was told I could dress and go home, but yet again Dr. Eliot wanted another view of my spine.

"I'd like to know the reason for all this morbid interest," I said, knowing nevertheless that they never tell you.

At last I was released, to wonder over a long weekend and a day or two beyond what had so fascinated the X-ray department. My imagination went a lot further than my medical information. It kept offering unwelcome suggestions.

I learned the facts from Dr. Bob after he had reported favorably as to other tests. I asked him directly about the X-rays as I was leaving his office.

"Your spine is loaded with arthritis," he said cheerfully. There was no reason for other than cheerfulness. I was my age and I had been aware of that all along.

This was not my first acquaintance with arthritis, as I feel I ought to acknowledge. Several years ago the little finger of my left hand decided not to straighten out of its own accord. It didn't hurt but it complained a little. Its lack of initiative and volition became a nuisance, not much of a nuisance, but for quite a while. Then suddenly after many months the finger became normal again, even spirited, and so it still is.

Since then my other little finger has been affected in the same way and so far shows no sign of a spontaneous recovery. I must do most of its work for it. An arthritic tendency shows up in other parts of my body also, though mainly I get along well and am content.

I don't know that my experience with arthritis so far has any significance beyond the common bond of age, but it supports Emerson's dictum that "old age is not disgraceful, but immediately disadvantageous."

⟨

Emerson was fifty-nine years old when he wrote his essay on Old Age.

⟨

Graham weighs eighty pounds. I know, because he needed pills for tapeworm and Les Freeman weighed him yesterday at the Foote Memorial Clinic of the Massachusetts S.P.C.A. I don't think any of Graham's four collie predecessors weighed more than seventy pounds, but Graham at eighty is compact, hard of muscle, and quick of response.

He was required to take five large pills. I tossed the first three down his throat in the approved manner, but by that time he lost patience and gobbled the others himself.

I weigh a hundred and sixty pounds, which I can say without credit to myself, yet pridefully, is about what I weighed forty years ago. I was born to be on the lean side, and I look forward to a skinny last chapter rather than a rotund or obese one. The genes will have it their way as they always do, though I believe in helping them along with as much outdoor, all-season walking as possible. Where else but to the genes may one look for information as to what a human past was or what a human future will be? Here is one of our modern necromancies.

Graham and I felt autumnal, and this was the day of our expedition to and beyond Ram's Hill, one of the highest hills in the north shore range of our Island, yet I think I have never seen the name on any map. Nathaniel Southgate Shaler, Kentuckian and Harvard geologist, who long ago acquired hundreds of acres in this region, including Ram's Hill, wrote: "If a mountain or hill goes about it aright, it can get an amazing dignity without assaulting the heavens in its efforts."

So it is with our Island hills, which seem so much higher than they are because they rise above the sea in spectacular contrast. Ram's, though, is cloaked with trees and you come upon it with some surprise unless you have long known where the ascent begins.

Shaler also wrote, under the same Island spell to which he responded so deeply: "It is the light from the past which gives these scenes their abiding dignity; but this light does not shine forth from the pages of the guide book; it must come from the ancient wealth of the mind." In forthright presumption I applied these words to myself, remembering Ram's Hill as it was in my boyhood, open to the sky, with a few cedars and thickets invading a dying pasturage; remembering also the epic of the glacier and its history recorded in the rugged landscape, with which long familiarity and affection had established in me some claim of intimacy or even kinship. We all try to make our experiences as private as we can.

The light from the past, however considered — my childhood or the age of ice — does shine brightly as I walk through these woods with Graham. We set out from our house, Fish Hook, and took the old road, a mere trail now, which leads past the underwater cranberry bog to Zeph's Hollow. My brother drove through here with horse and buggy in the early days of the century, and how long ago that was the tall trees now boast.

No cranberries in the Underwater Bog now — the name occurs in old deeds, and despite a dry summer the water stands high and black against the banks. An old drainage ditch has been clogged since the time of my boyhood when we would pick a barrel of cranberries of an afternoon, and how my mother made jelly of them all I can't imagine.

We came to the boundary stone wall and the gully through which my brother's buggy wheels used to rattle and scrape. Here begins the smooth track of Zeph's Hollow, a level passage left by the glacier in a landscape otherwise distinguished by hills, boulders, ravines, and broken ridges. We never knew who Zeph was, and I imagine even his name will soon be lost, there is so little now to tie the past to the present. Our past, I mean. The glacial past is reclaiming its own.

We turned aside from the hollow and began to climb the steep slope of Ram's Hill as my brother and I did long ago. The path leads steeply upward with few arrests, an ascent of much more than a hundred feet accomplished in less than a quarter of a mile. The path twisted a little, as if to gets its breath. So old are the woods now that we encountered little underbrush.

We were soon at the top, although one might doubt which among three peaks is the real summit. Graham, who had been ranging from side to side in exploration, stood with me while I beheld the view. He tasted the higher, fresher air with long tongue and nostrils, watching me sidewise as if in tolerance but also in sharing. Through leafless treetops I could see a long expanse of Vineyard Sound, sleeping blue strait; and more distantly on the other and far side of the Island, the different blue of Old Ocean reaching to a secret haze against the sky.

I remarked to Graham that in a not too pretentious way we might consider ourselves on a peak in Darien. He gave me an extra sidewise glance, appreciating as always that we were engaged in a common enterprise even though he did not know precisely what it was. He went on tasting the air and finding it good.

On its eastern flank, Ram's Hill falls away more precipitously than on any other. One peers over a sudden brink and is tempted to say that the prospect is straight up and down. Yet from top to bottom of this sheer hillside the pioneers built a stone wall that stands firm today as in the beginning, gravity holding higher rock against lower rock, and the entire wall against the earth. Like all Vineyard stone walls, this is built of mixed boulders as well as of rocks and lesser stones, the boulders as often in the middle or near the top as at the bottom. I wondered whether any wall, depending on weight and balance, without mortar, could ever have been built closer to the perpendicular.

We moved on, pausing on each of the next two peaks, and then went down on the southwestern side, a longer and gentler descent through the woods. We turned when we reached the Old Schoolhouse Road and traversed the whole distance of Zeph's Hollow, broad and level. Three white-tail deer waved their banners at us as they quickly vanished.

We were soon back at Fish Hook. The exploration, I knew, had done me good and had been much to Graham's advantage also. We both profit by the outdoors, by exercise, and by the spirit of past-into-present, although this last is of less concern to Graham. He has visited Ram's Hill less often than I. It was in my thought now that my debt to him was considerable, since without him I should not have made the exploration at all.

In the evening I read Emerson's essay on Nature, the first time in several years. I found the prose shrewd and luminous but was put off by it as I am never put off by Thoreau.

"The cool disengaged air of natural objects makes them enviable to us, chafed and irritable creatures with red faces," Emerson wrote, "and we think we shall be as grand as they if we camp out and eat roots; but let us be men instead of woodchucks and the elm shall gladly serve us, though we sit in chairs of ivory on carpets of silk."

Emerson was no inspector of snowstorms, self-appointed or otherwise, and it was of the least importance whether he was present at the rising of the sun.

～

Thirty years or so ago I suffered a duodenal ulcer due to the anxieties of foreign travel, so much greater to me than its satisfactions. I could not make myself at home in the southern hemisphere where water runs out of a sink a different way, the southwester substitutes for our roaring northeaster, and there is no star to mark the North Pole.

Other reasons were doubtless more important, but these are more literary.

Dr. Clement Channing Nevin — "Chan" we all called him — who was the uncle of the present Dr. Bob, said that "the chronicity of ulcers is well recognized." I remember his phrasing exactly. He was, of course, correct, and at times when the spring or autumn flood of memory sets upstream in Conrad's River of the Nine Bends, ulcer symptoms visit me again.

I yielded some ground to them this fall, and a friend suggested that I counter with what is known as Transcendental Meditation, a program that I know to be based on sound principles and the effectiveness of which is established by objective tests. Why, then, did I fail to follow my good friend's advice?

Well, partly because Transcendental Meditation must begin with a ritual of lighted candles, and partly because I did not like the look of the guru whose picture appeared on the circular. Such is the nature of prejudice. But my genes were at fault too, for they and I all like to be out in the weather.

A New Englander is capable of observation, contemplation, and at times even of serious thought, but these faculties do not function well when he is in a state of idleness. Watch how he fidgets at a meeting. Shut up within walls, he frets, and often he frets when he is closed in by conventions. That is what I know I would do while enduring a period of Transcendental Meditation. How many minutes more? How soon can I get out of this? How quickly can I get back to all the things I have planned to do — and to the things that have just now, since I am idle, occurred to me? I am not a fit subject. It seems to me that even relaxation must be sought for and earned, not imposed by instruction from the outside.

Mind and body do constitute "the seamless web" of which Stanley Burnshaw has written with the amplitude of fascinating references and authorities. The theme of *The Seamless Web* relates particularly to the authorship of poetry which is of the organism entire, and not of any separatist segment, but it invites extension and the widest application.

I take it, too, that my ideas, such as they are, improve for being out in the climate. Meditation comes to me afoot, such as it is, and I often find myself refueled when I arrive home. This is no doubt often an exercise in escape, but escape is better than fretting or brooding. Meditation of the higher and purer sort is so remote a goal that I am not up to its pursuit. I have found a similar difficulty in public or private intervals of silent prayer. My mind wanders and I become curious as to what others present are saying to themselves before the concluding "amen" sets them free.

∽

Graham wanted to go out at 2:32 this morning, one of the least convenient of times. I can report exactly because last year I acquired a digital clock radio with a pale green gleam that eavesdrops on me and boasts of the time with spectral authority. Digital devices are all the thing nowadays, and George-Henry Madeiros is going to sell me a digital calculator, something almost on the order of a computer, so that at this late chapter I will be able to balance my checkbook and bank statement.

As to Graham, I think his manner of waking me is of some interest. He came into my room and dropped an article of underwear beside my bed. This was a matter of ritual value known only to him. Then he went to the staircase, descended three steps, sat on the widest where the staircase makes a space-saving turn, and waited. He waited in silence, something I found it difficult to bear. Is there anyone else who has tried to compose himself to sleep while his dog waited on the third step down from the top?

He can make quite a clatter when he chooses, so that the suspension of all sound was obtrusive. He engendered a state of suspense more shattering than a broadside of artillery. If I am in my soundest sleep, when Graham takes up his third-step post I am instantly aware of something begun and left unfinished, something that must be attended to. In no drowsy condition but fully awake, I attend to it.

He looks up at me in the light that now floods the hall, and seems to say, "Of course you're coming. I knew you would."

I HAVE LONG KNOWN, a lesson taught more than once by experience, that when a person dies, a signal is set at the courthouse that an occasion for free plunder has come again. An estate goes only in part to the heirs named in a last testament. By the act or non-act of dying the devisor has arranged an event something like a shipwreck around which claimants little known until now will gather around for a share of salvage.

The fact that legalism cloaks this performance does not make it any more acceptable for the aged and aging to contemplate, especially when they have won through to a modest accumulation of funds by years of hard work and discipline, and would prefer to pass on the benefits to persons or institutions of their own choice.

And so I have tried to attain a Byzantium (that country

for old men as Yeats saw it) of my own by transferring some of my funds into annuities. The agreeable side of this is that the rate of return is high, better for me than thirteen percent, as I figure in my Parker Street School arithmetic; the disagreeable side is that the actuaries obviously do not think highly of any long survival on my part. A factor of major importance is that almost seventy percent of the annual return is not taxable for purposes of the federal income levy, though regrettably this means it is largely my own money coming back to me.

My regret is offset a good deal by the fact that if my money gives out while I am still alive, the insurance companies will pay me out of their own funds as long as I survive. Don't worry, my accountant said to me, they protect themselves. Of course they do, and all lawyers overcharge, but my vitality may possibly outrun their actuarial prudence. If I can keep going for two more years, at least one company will have me on its dole. This is all I understand at present of the annuity principle.

Except, of course, that my heirs will be done out of some of the gleanings that might be left to them after the lawyers and the I.R.S. have finished with my estate. But my heirs are nephews, grandnephews, and grandnieces, to whom the taxing authorities wouldn't let me leave much, anyway. I can do more for them, if I last a while, by assisting them while I am alive, and the annuity income will make all the difference.

One step in their behalf I have taken by setting up an *inter vivos* trust as recommended by the author of *How to Avoid Probate*, the book that drove the legal profession into conniption fits. A lawyer likes to count upon his mortuary revenues.

I picture a scene that is likely to take place after my death, witnessing it here ahead of time since I must be absent from the real event. The appraisal of my estate has been made, and the appraisers have been paid. Their account is in the hands of the attorney charged with responsibility for the legal processes of my estate. The Internal Revenue Service will decline to accept the appraisal, raising the figures just enough so that it will not pay to take an appeal to the courts.

Presenting himself to my nephew-executor at a time suiting his purpose will be Mr. Jaggers, the attorney, nicely dressed, his hands in his pockets, his back to the warmth of the afternoon sun.

"The minimum fee of the Massachusetts Bar Association," Mr. Jaggers will remark with matter-of-factness, "is three percent of the probate value of the estate."

He lets it be understood that three percent is what he intends to charge, without reference to the services he may or may not have performed. He is not apologetic. He is talking only about the minimum. How much higher might he not go if he felt like it? And three percent sounds so small — just three cents on the dollar. My executor-nephew is relieved at being let off so easily. He has no fault to find with the authoritative Mr. Jaggers, and certainly not with the Massachusetts Bar Association, which wouldn't engage in price-fixing if it were not legal.

My executor-nephew has not discovered fully what inflation has done to the dollar, or what the appraisal in its final figures has done to the generally accepted value of the estate. The value has escalated, and so has the three per cent. Happily my *inter vivos* trust has removed a good bit from the probate amount, but that's all my nephew has going for him.

Mr. Jaggers is an estimable and indispensable figure in our society, but it takes a lot to support him in the style to which he is accustomed. I dislike the thought that my estate might have to bear an unnecessarily large part of the burden.

⌒

My attic, although young as New England attics go, has inherited increasingly through the years, all without recourse to the probate court. I cannot guess the origin of much of the accumulation of chattels and materials that must have come down in the family from its different branches in times past. No testament seems to have been required. The stuff just showed up.

It is usually too cold or too hot for comfort in my attic, and the roof slopes so sharply that I risk bumping my head. Some fortitude is therefore required of me to look over the things that have wound up in so unlikely a place. No receipt required. For every arrival, only the chance of some departure in an uncertain future.

Betty used to say that we shouldn't leave the attic full of things — she may have said "junk" — for our heirs or other latecomers to dispose of. I too subscribed to this principle, but ground-floor decisions fade into hesitation and surrender up under the roof. All power of disposal is atrophied.

Those old suitcases, scratched and worn, are of better appearance than I had thought. They will surely "do" for a few more times. But "do" for what? I have no idea. Nothing is more remote from my inclination than to travel even as far as the mainland, and if I go to Boston to see the oculist in April as usual, it will be of the first importance for me to arrive home the same night. The overcoat on the hanger just beyond the skylight, ragged and partly dismantled by time, has nevertheless a sheep's-wool lining one can't duplicate today. Is it possible that someone might transfer the lining into a different coat?

The trunks, for decades idle, have gathered a patina of dust. What use for trunks anymore? But they were worth a good deal once, and to throw them out would be to violate the trust of an old account. Memories will swing the balance here and almost all along the line.

And the books! They must go, for they have been looked over and looked over again, handled and rehandled. The decision has been made, followed by reprieve after reprieve. That copy of *Rebecca of Sunnybrook Farm* — Aunt Addie gave it to me for Christmas once, unaware that it was hardly apt for a boy's reading. Now it has a lonely association with that dear old woman. Aunt Henrietta is represented here also — the tarantula's nest, the horsehair lariat, the clay head that, sprinkled with grass seed, would grow whiskers, the china duck. Everything is here except the horned toad that got away.

I turn to the stranger books, alien volumes of mysterious origin. An 1818 copy of *Essays Moral, Economical and Political* by Francis Bacon is devoted to "Apothegms." A sample:

> 60. One came to a cardinal in Rome and told him that he had brought his lordship a dainty white palfrey, but he fell lame by the way. Saith the cardinal to him, "I'll tell thee what thou shalt do; go to such and such a cardinal — naming him half a dozen cardinals — and tell them as much; and so whereas by thy horse if he had been sound thou could have pleased but one, with thy lame horse thou mayest please half a dozen."

And another sample:

> 250. Bion was sailing, and there fell out a great tempest; and the mariners that were wicked and dissolute fellows called upon the gods, but Bion said to them, "Peace, let them not know you are here."

I don't know whether age is a qualification for making up apothegms but I fancy it is, assuming a certain amount of sense accumulated along the way, so I produce a few almost offhand:

36. Thunder is well known to be a frightening phenomenon to country people and some are put to it for recourse when a storm impends in open country. Eliphalet, seeing a girl home from a party and being aware of heavenly artillery at no great distance, found a convenient means of avoidance. Having arrived at a stile, he inquired of his companion, "You know where you live, don't you?" "Yes," said the girl, and Eliphalet rejoined, "Then hoof it."

890. Josiah, a wise man in his middle years, was reduced in age to the lowly occupation of emptying privies. Having been summoned by a lady of ample means to estimate a figure as the cost of his services, he showed that acumen had not departed from him. Looking closely into the vault, he observed, "You live well, you do."

65. Mary Ellen, having been confined to a hospital bed for two weeks, remarked to a visiting friend, "My daughter brings me a bouquet of violets every day." Said the visiting friend, "My, you must be tired of violets."

The numbers here are fictitious, as in the instance of a new business firm engaging in trade for the first time and ordering its checkbooks to be numbered with 500 for a beginning.

I am in no hurry now to throw out those old books. The attic chill is less formidable today, or perhaps I am accustomed to it and it becomes a kind of protective privacy, as when George and I were allowed to play under the eaves at Fish Hook on a rainy summer day.

I sit on a corner of a steamer trunk, circa 1910, where light strikes well from a western attic window. Another small volume near at hand is *The Ingoldsby Legends*,

London, Richard Bentley, MDCCCXL. This wasn't the edition I knew as a boy when I laughed over "The Jackdaw of Rheims." I open at a random page:

"These lands," continued the antiquary, "were held in grand serjeantry by the presentation of three owls and a pot of honey — "

"Lassy me, how nice!" said Miss Julia. Mr. Peters licked his lips.

"Pray give me leave my dear — owls and honey, when- ever the king should come a rat-catching to this part of the country."

"Rat-catching!" ejaculated the squire, pausing abruptly in the mastication of a drumstrick.

"To be sure, dear sir: don't you remember that it once came under the forest laws — a minor species of venison? 'Rats and mice, and such small deer', eh? Shakespeare, you know. Our ancestors ate rats." ("The nasty fellows!" shuddered Miss Julia in a parenthesis) and owls you know are capital monsters" —

"I've seen a howl," said Mr. Peters, "there's one in the Sohological Gardens — a little hook-nosed chap in a wig — only its feathers and — "

Mr. P. was destined never to finish a speech.

"*Do* be quiet!" cried the authoritative voice, and the would-be naturalist shrank into his shell, like a snail at the Sohological Gardens.

"You should read Blount's 'Jocular Tenures', Mr. In- goldsby," pursued Simpkinson. "A learned man was Blount! Why, sir, His Royal Highness the Duke of York once paid a silver horse shoe to Lord Ferrers . . ."

"I've heard of him," broke in the incorrigible Peters. "He was hanged at the Old Bailey in a silk rope for shoot- ing Dr. Johnson."

Dr. Johnson shot? What a startling idea as to the Great Cham of literature who, so far as I know, died a natural death at the age of seventy-five, a pretty fair example for the longevity of such as I. I pause. I am being laggard with minutes which make up hours which make up days which make up Time. But it is hard to leave off with such a conversation uncompleted — symbolism so forthright and unashamed. Nothing covert here, new faces of consciousness coming up crisply and brightly as shuffled cards.

Nevertheless I glance out the window and see Graham at the postern gate below, quietly diligent, not without thought of passing cars or the oilman or his friend of the United Parcel Service. Although the attic is only two stories above the ground, the height, the separation between me and Graham, seems tremendous and revealing. I remember this same effect of seeing afar and from on high when I sat at my desk in Miss Rose Meaney's room on the second floor of the Parker Street School. It was she who taught me to multiply numbers in my head, though only simple numbers.

I liked Miss Meaney because she was young and pretty, but nevertheless I gazed out the window and gained a slant, angular view of earth and its affairs, separated off, the people going about their business unaware that they were being observed. From a perch only a few degrees elevated, one puts proportion upon the life from which one is selectly apart. I was the secret observer. That view helped me a little in becoming a convinced individualist.

The sight of Graham calls to me. A notice served, not too much unlike the warning on the old Fall River boats in ceremonial steamboating days: "All ashore that's going ashore." I must return to the world.

~

Yesterday afternoon a young woman called on me during her rounds of taking the town census. Graham ushered

her in from the front gate and stood listening to our interview.

She verified my age and citizenship, showing no surprise
at either. Then she asked how many lived in my house.

"Just the two of us," I said.

Like Abou Ben Adhem's angel, she wrote in her book
and vanished. I expect her again next year.

∽

I shared a banana with Graham before we set out on an
afternoon expedition. I had realized that the day would
be a good one for looking for lost things. The chill of early
morning had relaxed and sunlight took warm control. At
a little past noon the sky had become partly clouded and
the air was suffused with a temptation to repeat old sorties.
The more I considered the matter, the more the day became
nostalgic, and the more certain I became of an appointment
to be kept or a quest to be resumed.

Looking for lost things: but I do not mean looking for
lost youth or lost years. We know where they are, and
nothing is really lost if you know where it is, even if it is
at the bottom of the ocean. Or so we boys used to say. I
know where my youth is, though it seems to drift a little
above the bottom of an ocean called time. Some of it can
be recalled for a while and then it goes back without any
will of mine to its proper place.

There are two sharp turns of the highway as it passes
through West Tisbury, and a while ago Colbert Smith
asked me which one was called Dead Man's Corner. I had
never heard either one called that, though I was not surprised by the question. Latecomers supply names for occasions or places back beyond their own recollection.

But I know at which corner young Phillips was killed
when his automobile failed to make the turn and smashed

up on a late August night in 1916. It was not the arbor
vitae corner nearest the cemetery. It was the race track
corner. It was where the road comes over the flats. This
was what North Tisbury used to call the level stretch of
land bordering for quite a distance on the great Whiting
Field where the race track used to be, with the lofty tim-
bered structure of the judges' stand, long weathered even
when I was a boy.

I know the right corner, because my brother George and
I had walked through the woods from Fish Hook especially
to see the races that day, which was the opening of the
three-day West Tisbury Fair. Captain George Fred Tilton
was to race his gray, Edgar M., and there was a lot of talk
about what he might do. But when we approached the
corner we saw a notice nailed to the rail fence, saying that
because of the tragedy at that spot the previous night the
races would not be held.

A group of bystanders talked in quiet voices, some going,
some coming, some staying because there was nothing else
to do. George and I hung around for a while, listening to
the talk, and then we walked home. We had never known
young Phillips and did not see what his death had to do
with the horse races that we had wanted to see. I never did
have a chance to watch George Fred's Edgar M. in action.

This is what I mean by reaching for the past, looking for
long unthought-of things. Not lost youth, but something
in my lifetime never found. Such as — on this particular
afternoon — investigating the remains of a lost civilization.

The sun was already lowering at three o'clock when
Graham and I reached Fish Hook and entered the woods on
the south, near where the old privy used to be, the one with
plastered walls and two diminutive holes for children. The
apple trees in which we had tree houses were long gone,
their place taken by brambles and thickets. Then we came

to the oaks, all bare of leaves, the ground covered with leaf-drifts where they had blown or fallen. Graham could tread on this autumn carpeting with hardly a sound, such is the delicacy of his motion, but I rustled a good deal as I walked. The leaves felt good under my feet.

I looked first of all for the site of the ancient sod house. Mayhew G. Norton, our North Tisbury neighbor, told us about it long ago on a summer evening at Fish Hook when I was too young to ask questions. What I understood was that the sod house had been built in early times and occupied by settlers of whom there had been no record left. Mr. Norton said the location was marked by a great flat stone that had been in back of the fireplace. As soon as I could I went looking for the great flat stone, but without finding it.

How long does it take an early civilization to disappear? Our Island was settled first in 1642, and I have supposed that the sod-house generation must have had its day in the sun soon after that, leaving time enough for it to flourish, decline, and disappear into forgetfulness a century or so before I was born. Mayhew G. must have known something of the story, but I have never found anyone else who did. His son Charles did not remember that he had said anything about it.

A small matter, probably, but not small in my childhood fascination or in my grown-up imagining. I suppose I had made a ghost story of it, the ghost being what I conceived as not only a composite of human beings but also of a way of life.

Mayhew G.'s only direction had been that the sod house stood beyond two tall, unfinished stone posts that formed a gateway to a deserted place of thickets and advancing trees. I knew well enough about those stone posts. They marked a gap in the wall on the far side of a hay field from Fish

Hook. The wall still stands, but the field has grown into tall oak woods. Once in my boyhood Antone Viera came from Vineyard Haven to cut hay in the field, and I can taste the sweet summer flavor now. My mother gave Antone a dipper of cold water from our cistern, and he stood at the wall smiling and drinking deeply. How hot it was that day! You can't buy such a dipper today, and I keep the old Fish Hook dipper on my study wall for memory's sake. A few years ago the *Vineyard Gazette* helped have one like it sent to the Museum of Science in Boston so that children now growing up can visualize how the dippers in the sky got their names.

George and I, as boys, explored beyond the stone posts where the ground fell away rapidly. Well sheltered at the bottom we found a great lilac bush and a stoned-up basin supplied by a brook that flowed from one swamp and disappeared into another. There was no cellar hole nor was there a stone slab. A dwelling had certainly stood here, and an old one, when hollows were sought for shelter, before anyone thought of building on a hill.

At the southern end of the field stood another pair of tall stone posts, but we knew the reason for them. They stood at either side of the road through the woods that led to the Ann Dunham place on Seven Gates Farm. We walked that road often, sometimes to pick mayflowers where the road became a path skirting a high oak bank on one side and a brook on the other. As years passed, the road and path became difficult to find, but once found, mayflowers were found also, still prospering in the same leafy place.

A year ago, after I had forced a way through the briars and bushes between these stone posts, hoping to trace the old road, I turned a bit to the left and came upon a slab of rock, not so great as I had fancied it would be, but great enough to show that here had stood the sod house of my early, forgotten civilization. The rock stood upright at one end of a hollow, almost filled with the accumulated fallen leaves of more years and generations than I could imagine. This hollow was clearly recognizable as a sort of cellar hole, though apparently the dwelling was of only one floor, depressed into the ground for shelter and greater warmth. There were no stoned-up sides, and I looked unsuccessfully even for that familiar mark of old life and custom, a worn stone doorstep.

So, as I say, on this new expedition looking for lost things, Graham and I, after entering the woods, first turned aside to visit the memorial setting of the forgotten sod house. We stood at the edge of the hollow, the silence poignant about us.

Then we set out to try again to trace the Ann Dunham road. Graham, instead of making his usual side excursions, or tracking ahead, stayed at my heels. I was the commander of the expedition, and in any case the afternoon was one for staying together. We were going where no one had been for half my lifetime, and before that there was no knowing who.

I turned a little aside to inspect a massive boulder with lichened shoulders, rising solitary among the trees. Near the boulder we came upon another hollow where perhaps there had been a dwelling or an outbuilding. I guessed, though, that in the period of sod houses there wouldn't have been outbuildings of any account. The mystery would continue, but I was adding to what I was unconsciously regarding as my private antiquity. Between me and those others, so much older and earlier, who had lived here, I felt a tie. This secret and lonely woodland had passed from them to me, even if on this one afternoon alone.

Presently I moved on, Graham following, and we came

by luck and the slightest of indications in the leaf cover, to the spot where the old road had crossed the brook. Partly through a threshold memory of boyhood, partly by instinct, and perhaps a little by the favor of destiny which sometimes holds in the smallest matters, I traced the route all the way to the lookout in the stone wall above the Ann Dunham place where I had last stood as a boy. I had completed my errand, and perhaps I felt a little as James Ramsay must have felt when at the end of the book he reached the lighthouse. Graham shared my satisfaction, though he had no idea of any reason for it.

The sky darkened except where some western color had begun to rise beyond the woodland. We were finished with the ghostliness of our expedition, and we walked back to Fish Hook without once losing the way. The coolness of the air became a fresher delight for both of us. Graham kept tasting it, but I had no idea what scents he detected, or what they meant to him.

We drove through the gloaming, thirteen miles back to Edgartown. The shop windows were lighted and despite the automobiles crowding the curbsides, the town seemed very old and very small. An ancient fitness seemed to linger as night settled in.

◇

I came across my father's "Standard Daily Reminder" for the year 1920, though how I happened to have it or how it turned up I cannot explain. Most of the pages are blank, but for some weeks there are many small notations. An item lacking proportion to the significance of the event recorded is this:

Tuesday, June 8, 1920. Went to New York via 11:45 a m and Knickerbocker. A.L.H., H.B.H., and G.A.H.

A.L.H. was my mother. No one would guess from this entry that I was bound for my wedding. This wasn't the way I remembered it, either. I thought that I had gone to New York by shore line, brooding all the way.

> Wednesday, June 9, 1920. In New York. Saw The Night Boat at the Liberty in the evening.

Well, we did see the musical show, *The Night Boat*, naughty by the standards of the time. I don't know whose choice it was. I felt put off by it; my morality was offended and my taste subjected to shock. I didn't care for *The Night Boat* on the eve of my wedding, and I was out of sorts because Betty sat with my father, and my mother and I sat behind them. He hadn't been able to get four seats together.

> Thursday, June 10, 1920. Marriage, H.B.H. and E.W.B. at Grace Church by Rev. Charles L. Slattery, rector. Left New York in the Commonwealth.
> Friday, June 10, 1920. Home from New York. Made quick connection Fall River and reached Campbell Street at about 8 a. m. Busy day at the office.

My father was always one for quick connections. The *Commonwealth* was the grandest, most costly, and most recklessly fated of the Long Island Sound steamers. She was built too late, after the crest of size and luxury in steamboating had begun to subside. Her seasons were short, else she would have bankrupted the company, and her era been even shorter.

But Betty and I were at Mohonk, in a period-piece hotel on a strange lake in the Shawangunk Mountains in upstate New York, though not far upstate, where snow had not yet melted from under some of the towering rocks. She and I were never to recall the same things in the same way. She thought the advertising phrase went, "where laurel lines the Mohonk paths in May" and I thought it went, "where laurel lines the Mohonk paths in June." Either way, I don't remember any laurel. Betty had brought along Upton Sinclair's *The Brass Check* and after our walks in the afternoon sat in a cerise robe reading it.

I don't think it rained while we were at Mohonk.

On Tuesday, June 15, 1920, my father wrote:

> H.B.H. and E.B.H. arrived via New Bedford Line. The six Houghs dined at Peters and went to the Olympia. Also Aunt Henrietta.

Anticlimax in concentrated form, and I guess it was much so at the time — an unremembered dinner and an unremembered movie at a theater. Was it one newly built where Ike Sherman's livery stable used to be, or was it the one beside the Old White Church and opposite the Parker House on Purchase Street? Only the slight peripheral shadow of Aunt Henrietta serves a halfway willingness to remember.

Betty and I had been met at the New Bedford Line wharf in the morning by Big Jack Frasier and his horse-drawn cab. Betty always said we took the cab as a sort of gag, but I think we took it for convenience, and that taxis were quite a new thing. In later years we were never sure how long we had stayed at Mohonk. My father clears that up, anyway.

Forgetting in the present is the easiest part. Forgetting in the past hangs over one like a misty dream. Betty and I lived all our married life with a deficit of solid information, which I guess didn't really matter. Now I, with those of my generation who survive, have my share of proprietorship in oblivion, not always to my regret, and that won't matter, either.

Cicero wrote that he had never heard of an old man forgetting where he had buried his money. Old men do forget exactly that, either literally or symbolically, and if at last they are able to remember, the recollection comes too late. They should never have buried it in the first place. Moments of shining beauty must be grasped while the day's sun is still high, or the night's moon. One hesitates to count on a rerun.

But I have known men who don't remember whether they buried any money but can recall exactly where they buried it and what the weather was like. They won't be pushed to go to the scene again, though. We live in an uneasy state until at last we are likely to remember nothing at all. We are apt to have turned off more faucets than we have turned on, and the tap is dry when we don't expect it to be. What remains is the sense of having lived, a sort of racial memory that carries on until the end.

The shadows of Plato's imagining on the walls of a cave, with their false picture of the outside world, have their counterpart in images we can see in broad daylight, not realizing that they are grotesques, distortions, or old ideas of our own. Are we not somewhat in a cave of our own making? What seems to be becomes more important than what is, and we should better have known that this was bound to be the case from our very beginning.

∽

I went yesterday to the small building behind police headquarters to apply for my identification card from the Martha's Vineyard Council on Aging. There was no ceremony whatever.

Hilda Gilluly, who was in charge, needed to ask me no questions, for she is the former Hilda Norton, daughter of Orin Norton, last of the Edgartown blacksmiths and old time craftsmen in the working of metal. He made our front-door latch out of a bronze propeller shaft.

Hilda and I remarked about old times, agreeing that we had the best of it, though my generation runs back before hers. Of course we had the best of it.

Then I returned to the car where Graham was waiting. The car serves about as much as his waiting room as it does for transportation.

❧

In the post office yesterday while I was attending to my mail at one of the front desks, I became aware that a man in line at the stamp window was behaving peculiarly. I discovered that Graham had begun leaping on him with all four feet above the floor. Evidently the man had spoken some words of greeting or kindness. Graham recognizes the amenities in this way, as if it were a sort of game. I had him on the leash, of course, and grounded him quickly. All the people in line understood Graham's good-natured fervor, but I was glad nobody sneezed. His response to sneezing began in early puppyhood and has matured with him into an active ceremonial.

The first thing necessary in understanding Graham's behavior is to realize that he has no wish to be human. Such an ambition has never occurred to him, and I have not suggested it. He is well off as a dog, and a dog he means to be.

A friend asks, "Why doesn't he want me to sit in this chair?" — or "pick up this paper" or "carry this package." Graham doesn't care a whit either way. It's anomalies that interest him, and he won't lose a chance for a demonstration over the smallest details if they are out of the ordinary course. Out of the ordinary for him is a variable concept which he plays in different ways according to his spirit at the time.

He also enjoys another high opportunity, that of recognition, and will push it to the utmost, all the better if something or someone previously known happens to turn up in the post office or the busiest block on Main Street.

Graham can distinguish subtle differences in all sorts of smells and sounds. He can judge how far off they are and often who is making them. I suppose he can identify the chemical composition of many substances, but for his own purposes, not ours, and he needs no names for them. He is sensitive to recurrences of all sorts, likes to anticipate them and to give them appropriate celebration. He is attentive to items he can see I consider significant, often revising his own judgments so that they go along with mine on the principle of sharing. He also occasionally matches or complements my behavior.

His sense of humor and mine overlap. If he absently runs into a tree or telephone pole while glancing backward over his shoulder, he looks at me with a glinting acknowledgment that the occasion is funny. His tail wags. We are on a common footing.

He can tell who has been where, and he can see in the dark, even if scent and memory help a good deal. I have known him to lope through utter blackness at night with his smoothest, fastest wave motion, though I think it has usually been a familiar blackness. The other evening at North Tisbury he charged away at high speed, and all I could see in the darkness was the white of his ruff as he veered this way and that. When he returned with a certain air of pride, expecting approval as always, there was no doubt that he had engaged slightly with a skunk.

Catherine Woodrow, Edie Blake, and I drove back to Edgartown with him in the back seat, all of us having placed too light a value on the quality of skunk fumes, no matter how attentuated. We shared the aftermath during the entire drive, and for weeks afterward the car smelled of that evening. Graham did not mind. He looked forward to a new day.

～

Today is Thanksgiving in the year 1974. Yesterday was the anniversary of my father's birth in New Bedford during the administration of President Andrew Johnson. Thanksgiving and my father's birthday invite that backward look so native to those who inhabit the territory of old age. Nostalgia has nothing to do with it in a basic sense. How can one help looking back at that long view? How else would we know how bad the present is? "The good old days" is a trite phrase, but here again it emerges, and those of us who are qualified to employ it properly can do so with a sense of authority.

The past does not stretch out seriatim, calendar leaf by calendar leaf, but in changing glimpses of a badly filed contemporaneousness. There's no system about it, no order, no nothing except the reenactment that seems to take place in the mind, along with loneliness, regret, romance, pleasure, and the sunrise and sunset colors. There's often a kind of serendipity about the associations that discover themselves with or without an apparent clue in reason.

On Thanksgiving and in the shadow of my father's birthday, I am sure I should like to go back if I could, but for one thing. I would have to be young again.

Emerson wrote: "There are always two parties, the party of the Past and the party of the Future, the Establishment and the Movement."

I didn't realize that the word "Establishment" was current in this meaning so long ago. Somebody seemed to have introduced it quite recently, and to have begun a vogue for which he won much public credit. With the "Movement" I have been familiar since early youth. Sometimes it has had to do with one thing and sometimes with another, its applications as varied as those attached to Coxey's army and fluoridation.

During World War II a companion of mine in the Naval Reserve Force in Washington was all eagerness to get back to civilian life so that he could throw himself into the Movement. I did not know what Movement he meant, but at the time no one would have dreamed of inquiring. The Movement, whatever it was, could always be assumed, and it was assumed, and taken seriously.

I profess to be a liberal, and at times I have been something of a revolutionary in an unarmed sense, but I admit that I must also belong to Emerson's party of the past. If I were younger I should object to his excluding a party of the present, but I now think he was quite right. The Movement I am involved in emotionally and to the extent of my powers is that of saving our planet from its course of destruction, though what I really want to save is the planet of yesterday which is already lost and gone. For its sake, nevertheless, I must press on.

My confidence in youth is as much as anyone's except youth's own, which is as it should be. But in spite of our wish that the situation might be otherwise, the major importance of youth is to itself, not to my generation or to any other already full grown, and an adversary relationship is not only inevitable but desirable. How else can there be any tautness of imminent change?

So I am estranged from those youths I might wish to join if I could, even at this late date. The most to be expected is an occasional flash of sympathy or understanding on either side.

Society spends vast sums to teach young people to live in

it, whereas youth will live in a society of its own making. Courses in social adjustment are therefore wasted substitutes for discarded liberal education. Most of what we spend is in the nature of bribery, anyway, and it never works. Ours is an easy age, and liberal education comes hard.

G<small>RAHAM ASKED</small> to be let out last night at a
few minutes past one by the clock. In my sleep I realized
naggingly that once again he had descended to the third
step of the staircase and induced a state of suspense that
brought me to the necessity of action. I threw my feet out
of bed, found my slippers and bathrobe, which took a good
deal of blind doing, and went into the hall.

There sat Graham, scrunched back a little, waiting with
confidence. But I did not think he looked as smug as usual,
and I may have kept him waiting overlong. We went the
rest of the way downstairs together, and I let him out by
way of the kitchen door.

He disappeared quickly from the limited glow of the
breezeway light, and I waited in sleepy patience for him
to show himself again.

Presently I became aware of him walking around in the moonlight as if he had nothing on his mind whatever. I envied him. Since I couldn't join him, I made him come indoors again and found that he didn't much object. Soon he was sound asleep on the bed in his room and I was tossing around on mine. René Dubos says, "Every organism, animal as well as human, lives in a private world of his own to which no one else has complete access." It's like the Old and the Young, but Graham and I are far closer in our worlds than they. We do have not only a companionship but common goals toward which we travel in a good spirit together.

〜

I have brought down from the attic an inlaid box of small size and agreeable proportions, made of different woods carefully joined and polished. The heat of many summers has cracked the varnish, which now in its crazed state appears old. The box was sent to me long ago by Eddie Tracey from the state's prison, where he was serving time for cracking the safe in the ticket office on the steamboat wharf at Oak Bluffs. Oak Bluffs is the traditional excursion town of Martha's Vineyard, a principal landing, and Tracey knew the Labor Day weekend would give him a good haul.

But he couldn't know of the romance between a young ticket seller and a hotel waitress of the resort town. In the course of business on the wharf, Henry changed a ten-dollar bill for Emily, giving her a five-dollar bill and five ones. On the five-dollar bill he wrote, "Keep This." But new bills had been issued that summer, and he decided to give her a new bill instead of the marked five-dollar bill, putting the latter into the cash drawer to keep for sentiment's sake.

The police were pretty helpless so far as tracing the safe-cracker was concerned, for there were no fingerprints and no other helpful clues. It just happened that Henry, the sentimental ticket seller, was a passenger on an Island steamer a day or so later and heard talk at the purser's window of a marked bill. He asked to see the bill, and undoubtedly it was his.

The man who had tendered the bill to the purser was named Carpenter, and he was, as the police quickly reported, "a convicted bootlegger." His story was that he had received the bill from a man he knew as Edward Kennedy, whom he had helped find a room in a house where he himself was domiciled for the summer. He said Kennedy had borrowed money from him at intervals and on the evening after the safecracking had repaid some of it.

This was enough to give the police a workable strategy. A state detective named Clemmey soon caught up with Edward Kennedy in Woonsocket, and it was now simple to prepare a case against him. He was Edward Tracey, alias Harry Kenney, Harry Tracey, Thomas W. Burns, Jack Martin, and Frank D. Fagin, names he had accumulated since 1917 at the rate of about one every two years.

Carpenter, to clear himself, must testify against Tracey, and it turned out that a man named Fisher might have been implicated if he had not become a hospital patient at the moment of action. When Fisher was no longer living, we saw him referred to as Rhode Island's Public Enemy Number One.

Tracey was charged with the safecracking and, high bail having been set, he remained all winter in the county jail at Edgartown awaiting the April sitting of superior court. Here was where time took its first turn of memorable slowness. The winter stretched on and on with leisurely days and weeks.

The county would have had Tracey transferred to some
other jail, but it couldn't. He had not been convicted. So
there he stayed, at our jail, and became friendly with the
jailkeeper's son and the son's schoolmates. The cells are
small, and Tracey had the liberty of the corridor a good
deal of the time, so that he could walk up and down. At
the end of the corridor he and the jailer's boy met and
talked.

At last in April he was brought to trial in the dignity of
the courthouse of the County of Dukes County, this being
the legal name our county bears. The judge's bench is of
shiny oak, and so are the stations of the sheriff and court
crier. Tall windows with venetian blinds admit long shafts
of sunlight which strike across the tiered benches for
spectators and the old-fashioned carpeting. Long patterns
of sunlight and shadow are related to slow time.

A jury was impaneled, and Carpenter, sullen informer,
told his story which was supported in important details by
Henry and Emily and the exhibited bill marked "Keep
This." The verdict was not much delayed. With Tracey
in the dock, his record was read in open court for the first
time: as Harry Kenney, July 30, 1917, arrested Brooklyn,
burglary, suspended sentence. As Harry Kenney, January
25, 1919, arrested Jefferson County, Ohio, breaking and
entering, received at Ohio State Reformatory March 7, on
sentence of from one to fifteen years. Paroled September
1, 1920, to New York City and granted final release October
21, 1921.

As Harry Peter Kenney, March 1, 1924, arrested Mt.
Vernon, New York, burglary. Sentenced to two years in
Sing Sing. As Edward Tracey, alias Harry Burke, attempt
to break and enter post office at Millville, Massachusetts,
March 22, 1926. Pleaded guilty and sentenced to three
years in the federal penitentiary at Atlanta. This brought

him to Martha's Vineyard and to our courtroom in April 1929.

The judge now imposed a sentence of not less than fifteen years and not more than eighteen years in state's prison. Spectators in the courtroom shuffled or rustled or drew in their breaths sharply at the sudden awareness of all this walled-in time. Years and years on end, life aging and changing in the outside air, but all normal life stopped short for Eddie Tracey.

He stood up and inquired, "May I say a word, your honor?"

The judge said he might, and he stepped forward, his face flushed, voice vibrant with passion.

"It is a pleasure at this time to express myself" — this attempt at good English came with an effort. "I made a great mistake when I did not take the stand. We have honor in all things and therefore I protected a woman's honor that I may suffer for something I know nothing about. I wouldn't borrow five cents from Carpenter, but one night I was intoxicated and I did borrow three dollars from him. I don't know where he got the marked five-dollar bill.

"I stand before you and raise my head to the solemn God above me that I never stole five cents in five years. I go to state's prison and smile with a bleeding heart."

Some of that five years must have been while he was in prison in Atlanta, even if his sentence had been shortened by parole. The judge, lean and incisive, magisterial in black robe, looked down from the bench.

"Your attorney has given you devoted and skillful service," he said to Tracey. "Had I been your lawyer I would not have put you on the stand with your record."

"If the state detectives told a straight story of all they know, I'd be innocent," Tracey shouted, pounding on the oaken rail. But what he really pounded against with all his strength was a wall of time. Years and years of time.

"I wish I had stolen the money. Do you think I'd be here? No, I'd be in Hong Kong or some other place," he shouted.

That was almost all. As he was led from the courtroom he saw the detective who had arrested him in Woonsocket.

"Good luck, Clemmey!" he yelled. "I hope you break a leg."

I have forgotten when the correspondence began, but Tracey was soon writing to us as he did to the jailer's boy. And the boy subscribed to the *Vineyard Gazette* for him, and renewed the subscription year after year. After an interval Tracey asked if he could write a column for the *Gazette* and we said he could try.

"For the past three years," his letter went, "it has been my pleasure to receive and read your interesting newspaper. I want you to believe me when I tell you that I look forward to receiving it every Friday morning when I come in from work."

He said he had written a radio drama and submitted it to the radio editor of the *Boston American*, who had praised it.

"Sir, all my life I have wanted to write. My first job was with the *New York Sun* as a copy boy. Perhaps you know my boss, Mr. Keating, who was editor at that time, also Mr. E. C. Hill, now a famous and favorite speaker on the radio, and now, after all these years I am working in the printing department of this bastille. So you will see, Sir, that I am right at home, that is, loosely speaking."

We might have printed some of Tracey's writings if they had been at all likely, but they were not. A small, adequate sample:

John Banana, a convicted bank thief, who had been caught red-handed with too many skins, sat reading one of the popular magazines in his prison cell. Banana's sentence read like a taxicab sign — ten and fifteen. His cell mate, Frank Wellington, an ex-school teacher, was asleep on the lower bunk. Wellington had been sentenced by that well known "Year Judge" — one year from now and you'll be out — for teaching the wrong lesson in evolution.

Banana had just finished reading an article on technocracy which told about substituting energy for gold.

John — What do you know about technocracy, Frank?

Frank, still half asleep — I never met him. When did he come in?

And so on, getting nowhere. But letters continued to come now and then from Eddie Tracey, the final one dated in January 1937:

About a month ago I was transferred to the Norfolk Prison from Charlestown. After spending six and a half years in Charlestown I can assure you that this transfer meant a great deal to me. Norfolk is an outstanding example of one of the most modern prisons in the United States. My entire outlook on life has changed. Here at Norfolk one is given the opportunity to improve physically as well as mentally. In the past six months I have gained six pounds and am in excellent health . . . I intend to take advantage of every opportunity to educate myself so that I will be fitted to take my position in the outside community and live as a good citizen.

I have often wondered if you realize what the *Gazette* means to me. I have read the paper for so many years that it seemed as though it has become a necessary part of my life. Therefore it is with the deepest sincerity that I extend wishes for your continued success and the hope of a joyously happy 1937 for you and your family.

Not only was this my last word from Eddie Tracey but it was to be the last I ever knew of him. Just when he sent me the inlaid box he had made in prison I do not remember. Of course I thanked him, and I telephoned the lawyer who had defended him, but there seemed nothing either of us could do. And so I put the box in the attic and forgot about it. Looking at it now, I can see a certain meaning in its emptiness. There was never anything to put in or take out.

I think of that slow-moving, almost arrested interlude of Tracey's winter in our jail, and then of the long years of his imprisonment, lost to us, and so gone as if overnight. Does a man age differently in prison as in theory he might on a spaceship bound into space? There's no answer that I can see, and the bare bones of chronology are the least of it.

෴

When vacation season comes to Martha's Vineyard each year with the advent of city people seeking sea air, recreation, and surcease, the taut fetters of time are relaxed. What a modern miracle this seems in each recurring June, for the restraint of time, though invisible, has become the harshest imperative we can know in the world. The harshness grows with each device technology provides for the economy of time, thus adding to the stress upon seconds, minutes, and hours. All the ingenuity of the ages has been used to serve the purposes of time — airplane, radio, telephone, check-out counter (though there's a lot of fretting and fumbling there), automobile, motorcycle.

And in June for a while the bonds are loosed. Men stand in the sunny mornings with nothing to do. Bankers loll on beaches. Executives, whether Mr., Mrs., Miss, or Ms., are seen in exotic colorful costumes with tennis rackets, golf clubs, highball glasses, oars, and so on. The very earth revolves more slowly. Science does not accept this principle but in relative terms it has truth within it.

Many of the vacationers, time-free — most of them, in

fact, sooner or later — admire the stone walls of the Vineyard which wind over hills, border old roadsides, or disappear into woodland which once was pasturage or tilth.
How, the wonder comes, did those early Islanders have
time for the patient labor and skillful building of these long
miles of stone walls? How, indeed?

Time was different then. So was money, but mostly
time.

So from the past the ancient ruins of clock-and-calendar-
kept accounts come down to our mostly enslaved generation. The wealth that was and is no more: time enough to
build by slow enduring labor the stone walls that stand, if
not as impressively as the monoliths of Stonehenge, then
hardly less so in their detail, workmanship, and record of
labor's time well spent.

This heritage of ours I call time's forgotten wealth, and
a hoard of it is contained in every Vineyard stone wall. I
think of this now and again, and it came to mind when I
was remembering Eddie Tracey's years in prison.

∽

Catherine Woodrow left this morning to take the seven
o'clock ferry for the mainland to spend the holidays with
her family. Her house is just beyond ours on the rim of
Sheriff's Meadow, and I saw her lights glowing when I got
out of bed a little after five-thirty. I lingered at breakfast,
and it was six-thirty before Graham and I were out in the
lane ready for the day's first circumambulation of the pond.

Graham heard the door of Catherine's car close and
called my attention to the sound. We waited a minute or
two while her engine warmed up, and then she drove past
us, headlights bright in the darkness. I waved as she went
by, and Graham slithered and wagged.

Now for a week or two we shall have only one light out

beyond us toward the pond. This matter of lights is far from perfunctory, and Catherine will understand when she comes back if I say, "We missed your lights" instead of saying "We missed you." This has a lot to do with age, for it is old people as a rule who have lived where lights were few and important, and the open country mysterious after the setting of the sun.

The town lights are collective, ours are individual and special, not commingled. Each has an identity and a degree of cheerfulness drawn from the heirloom past. A single star shows the direction of the North Pole, a single star guided the Magi, and a single gleam through old panes of glass can be translated into epics of human aspiration and solidarity.

There are other simple things of a like sort. We didn't think when we built our house that we were shutting off Miss Leila Pease's view of the town clock. Not that the town clock kept good time, or that Leila Pease in her advanced age lacked clocks and a radio of her own, but the town clock was company. It was there.

Graham likes to walk under the hedges on the other side of Sheriff's Lane, letting the twigs mildly scratch his back. I brush him when I remember, but this hedge-walking is his own idea and a preferred variation.

We have a row of box bushes he can use if he wants to. He often does. They grew from slips planted by my Aunt Henrietta in the garden of what was my grandfather's house in Vineyard Haven. After she died we moved them to Edgartown, where they have flourished into a genuine pride of box bushes, withstanding winter cold, snow, and sun, and scenting the air when warm days come.

My Aunt Henrietta was the one who married a Scotsman and lived in San Francisco for many years, later moving back home and subscribing to the *San Francisco*

Chronicle. Once she said to me that there was reason to believe she had first been named Henrianna and the name changed later on. She asked me to look up the records in the courthouse but the courthouse didn't have them. She was born after 1850 so her name is not printed in the Massachusetts Vital Records, and I guess I will never know any more than she did whether she was first christened Henrianna.

These comments are intended to represent the discursiveness of the old, of whom I am now one. We start out talking about a box hedge and wind up speculating about an aunt who may have borne an odd name.

◠

Now they are taking down the Christmas trees and lights on Main Street, and for a little while I shall miss them. They stretch now, after additions from year to year, all the way from Memorial Park and the jail to the block below the bank, drugstore, and liquor store at the Four Corners. There are no more corners at that intersection than at any other street crossing, but the landmark term originated in Edgartown long ago and continues to be cherished.

The town is brightened at the Christmas season. It is good to look up and down Main Street in the evening after supper, when Graham and I take a walk to observe vistas of trees and colored lights keeping the annual observance as they were meant to do. Sometimes we meet only one or two pedestrians like ourselves; and only a car or two, or briefly none at all, may be parked against the curb. It is like being alone with Christmas, an experience worthwhile.

The intention years ago was to keep cheer alive for shoppers in the evenings of December, but few shops kept open. Now there are only one or two. So the dollars-and-cents side has been adjourned, and the tryst of lights and spruces is for the purpose of Christmas alone. We know that, and value it accordingly. Wherever we walk, we are at home, for nothing seems pretentious.

Now, with Christmas gone, I have been trying to make a list of things that are not so much fun as they used to be. I thought the list might serve as a kind of stock-taking, and that it would probably stretch out for a number of pages. What else can be true of age if most of the fun of life is not past? Yet my list turns out to be short, and I don't think it is particularly interesting. Perhaps this discovery alone is worth the effort and may be thought of as a nugget to be put away with others in a collection.

I had no difficulty to begin with:

1. Meetings.
2. Spending a week in New York City — or a day or a night.
3. Journeying anywhere, even to Woods Hole, which is a ferry trip of about forty minutes.
4. Going to the movies.
5. Thanksgiving.
6. Christmas.

I have been told that I am becoming eccentric, but all the same as I read over these items my uppermost feeling is that of a good riddance. Something else may occur to me later, but at the moment I cannot add to the list. I can think of nothing else, except of course the many things no longer extant that were a good deal of fun in their day — circus parades, for instance.

Katharine Cornell is no longer on the stage, and the kind of play I liked best is described as "dated." All right, so am I, and thank heaven I don't have to be fond of the experimental theater. Chekov was avant-garde enough for me. William Powell and Myrna Loy are no longer in the movies, and neither, I think, is Claudette Colbert.

The side-wheel steamer *Uncatena* has sailed to the wharves of the morning or been broken up for junk, whichever way you look at it. A police station stands where my Uncle Ben's house used to be. Baseball has gone national, the same thing as being gone — for one who remembers Rabbit Maranville and his celebrated basket catch on the old Athletic Field in New Bedford.

Simply being young is also one of the things gone for good, and therefore doesn't rate the list. But I don't believe it would again be nearly as much fun as it was at the beginning of the present century. I can't prove this and would be disinclined to try.

I know better than to challenge the dogmatism and determined anti-sentimentality (even though the sentimentality is still so plainly there) of the modern world, especially the intellectual part, for it is intolerant of backward looks by men and women who are now in the years of aging. All one has to say is "I remember," and present-day critics and commentators fly into a dither. Remembering "way back when" is a rebukable exercise.

Yet when the slippage of years has spread our continents of time more widely apart, and more generations have gone on, enterprising researchers will seek some narrow treacherous passage across the gulf to dig into our middens, and by artifacts and yellowed papers, joined together with much hypothesis, try to reconstruct some image of what we were really like. We would gladly have told them all, and so saved them the trouble, if they had been willing to listen. But eras must wait their turn to come into fashion, and time must pass before they do.

There is a retort we can make to the young, even the intellectual young, though they are unlikely to spare much of their attention. Apollodorus said or wrote it first, and I borrow from him as from a source well tested by centuries.

He was born in Sicily and, it is said, flourished as a comic poet between 300 and 200 B.C.

"Do not despise, Philinus, the habits of the old, to which, if thou reachest old age, thou will be subject. But we, father, are greatly inferior in this. If a father does not act kindly, you reproach him in such language as this — 'Hast thou never been young?' And it is not possible for the old man to say to his son, 'Hast thou never been old?' "

As to my list of things that are not so much fun as they used to be, Thanksgiving and Christmas are easily disposed of. In their festival character they are of greater immediacy to the young — the younger the better — than to the old who have lived past so many of them with lengthening perspectives. The distilled joy of Christmas is a perishable phenomenon, and I find it almost enough now to stand alone with Graham, looking up and down Main Street with all its lights under a dark winter sky.

There is happiness remaining in both holiday seasons, but the ripe in years approach such pleasures more slowly and only after overcoming many obstacles and speculations. Fun is not exactly a habit of adult life, and too much of it may grate. A touch of serendipity is worth more than a glut of contriving.

The exploitation inherent in life today has tarnished all sorts of innocence, not least the innocence of Thanksgiving and Christmas. Neither, I think, could have been completely comfortable in an urban civilization anyway. Innocence needs space, distance, and a state of grace. Sophistication is no better than moist rot, the worse because it is irreversible. The only way it can be reconciled with innocence, and often with Christmas, is to make a cartoon out of what once was solemn, Disney fashion, and pretend that one is seeing around it on all sides, and laughing it off, though not quite. The sophisticated will also grow old, and in age there is a simplicity that comes again, a sort of new innocence after illusion and disillusion alike are over.

I notice that I have put meetings first on my list, and I suppose this is because I feel strongly about them. They are one of the worst forms of gregariousness, and people who go to meetings would be better advised to stay home. There are exceptions, and I suppose much depends upon one's definition of meetings.

I do not think that weddings and funerals are to be considered primarily as meetings, though they approach the dangerous edge a good many times; and it is necessary to have meetings of boards of selectmen, boards of appeal, county commissioners, boards of directors and such, all of them to be classed as institutional. There is seldom any way of escaping them or escaping from them with a whole skin, by which I mean in the aggregate the skin of our social order. Lodge meetings are in a category of their own, rising and falling with the level of civilization, and in our part of the country they have tended to diminish.

As a boy I was greatly taken with political rallies, and went to many of them in New Bedford in excitingly atmospheric halls in different parts of the city, but halls nowadays tend to be pretty much the same, and so does oratory, and I have lost the old spirit. Radio and television have also made a good deal of public discussion into a rite, with technological conformity dominant. Old-time vocabularies long ago became corrupted. I think that if I could be sure of hearing an old-fashioned blatherskite again, it would be worth a trip downtown on a cold night, but otherwise a good book is better.

I once addressed street-corner rallies in New York City in support of Robert M. La Follette, the valiant, the Fighting Bob of Progressive and World War I years, when he was running for President as candidate of the League for Progressive Political Action. Headquarters sent me out along with a veteran campaigner who always addressed his auditors in this style: "Ladies and Gentlemen, Fellow Sufferers from a Government of Special Privilege and Monopoly." The way he rolled this out, it sounded so fine that I almost envied him. But not quite. After a few nighttime corner speeches I withdrew.

One night Betty and I went to hear Fighting Bob himself address his followers in the old, old Madison Square Garden, the one that really was at Madison Square. He wasn't old. I believe he was only sixty-nine but something had diminished him, either time or a gulf in his life. His mane shone white and his zest was great, but his utterance lacked both fire and variety, his tale seemed twice-told, and his audience melted away, slowly at first and then like the ebb of an ocean tide. The pushing aside or overturning of chairs or just the exit noises were like water sucking over a stony shore. Betty and I stayed to the end, but sadly.

I have been to almost no political meetings since then, and those I have attended I have been able to forget, as I have been able to forget the tabernacle gatherings of Billy Sunday, the evangelist whose name was once greater than Billy Graham's is now.

The first public meeting I attended professionally was the annual gathering of the Non-Resident Taxpayers Association in the Martha's Vineyard resort town of Oak Bluffs. The non-residents, who came only in summer, felt they were not fairly treated. A Mr. Heywood complained about the rum bottles thrown on the grounds of the Episcopal Church. There was no local prejudice against this church, but it happened to be conveniently situated. Why should a bibulous vacationer take the trouble to walk the length of Circuit Avenue to reach the grounds of Sacred Heart, or even to make a side trip into the Methodist Camp Ground, when he could so easily throw his empty bottles into the front yard of Trinity?

A Mrs. Riddell said she was nearly driven out of her cottage five days a week by the baseball games played in Waban Park, upon which her parlor and balcony looked out at close quarters. A Colonel Corson — no meeting is complete without a retired military man — said he would be glad to have the ball games shifted to Hartford Park so that he could enjoy watching them. He was quite safe, for Hartford Park lacked room even for a good throw from the mound to home plate, much less a deep fly to left field.

The town water system, a private enterprise, came in for a drubbing. Mr. Treat, proprietor of a tutoring school, a man of presence, said he had ninety-two different complaints against the water rates and service. "I'm a pretty good lawyer," he went on, "and I've been fighting the water company tooth and nail for years. They can't turn off your water. Don't mind their regulations."

There's always a rouser who says they can't, but they always can, whether "they" are a water company, a lighting company, or a board of public something or other. Years later at a meeting of this kind I asked the principal rouser whether he was a lawyer. "No," he said, "but I am very well versed in legal procedure."

The most such a meeting can come to is the passing of resolutions to which a minority of those present are usually opposed, and which never amount to anything.

A year after my first taxpayers' meeting I went to the same room upstairs over a fire station to attend another annual meeting, but only one or two taxpayers showed up. Indignation had waned during the year or there was some counterattraction. The secretary, who for convenience was a town resident, closed his record book with a bang and made his way to the staircase chuckling. He was a large man, nicknamed "Porpoise."

The most recent meeting I attended was not by choice,

for it was held at my house. Graham was present also, and so were a dozen or fifteen concerned citizens who expressed their views tangentially, radiating outward like the spokes of a wheel, so that they would never meet, short of infinity, if then. Afterward several remarked that it had been a good meeting and that everyone had expressed himself freely. But nothing happened. Everyone took his own views home with him, and I kept mine too.

The other items on my list of things that aren't fun any longer seem to me self-evident. I liked to travel to New York by boat or Shore Line express, and one can't any more. The Fall River Line and other Long Island Sound lines were suspended long ago, and the shore route by train is said to be insufferable. I haven't tried it lately, because New York is not safe any more. I read the other day that although everyone there hasn't as yet been mugged, everyone knows someone who has been mugged or raped.

I was well acquainted with New York City in the administrations of John Purroy Mitchel, Red Mike Hylan, and Jimmy Walker. Betty and I used to walk to our hotel through dark streets after the theater, and we felt that the freedom of the city was ours. I did go back once or twice during the Lindsay era but felt lucky to get home intact. There was a strain in the very atmosphere. I'm not of an age to take chances, and I prefer to stay home with Graham even if I miss some new and unintelligible play.

I know it is unfair to put travel on my list because I never did enjoy it much except for trips on the Fall River boat. If I had a hundred dollars for every time I've been seasick between Vineyard Haven and Woods Hole, or in Buzzards Bay, en route to or from New Bedford, I would be rich, except for inflation. On the Long Island Sound steamers there might be rough seas off Point Judith, but one could always get into one's bunk.

I made my first passage in an airplane last summer at the age of seventy-seven. I had hoped to complete my life short of any experience whatever with the air age, but circumstances were such that I yielded. I was not nearly old enough to qualify for the usual news item about some old person going up for the first time and coming down in a superannuated glow of the adventure. I did not have any sense of adventure, and there was no occasion, physically or psychically, for me to glow.

I think I had postponed my flight to exactly the right point — aviation was obviously fully developed. My friend Mac at the Martha's Vineyard airport passed on the word that I was a first-time passenger and entitled to V.I.P. treatment. This is what I got, even to having some club or other at Logan Airport opened before the usual Sunday hour so that I could wait in grand surroundings for my TWA flight. And I was punctiliously seated next to a window on the big plane. Friends have asked me what kind of plane it was, expecting me to identify it by its type number. I have no idea what the number was. I know only that it was big, and as steady in flight as I had been assured it would be.

I implaned at Boston and flew to St. Louis in two and a half hours. There it was — St. Louis, on the Mississippi River, as I had always understood but had more or less forgotten. It formerly required three hours to get from Woods Hole to Boston by train, and the trip nowadays by automobile seldom takes more than two hours.

The luncheon served by TWA was as good as that at Massachusetts General Hospital, I thought, and the occasion superior. If Betty could have been along, we would have been participants together in something like Ring Lardner's "Golden Honeymoon" story, with the same blend of naiveté, novelty, innocence, and rather self-conscious sophistication. But I don't think Betty would have flown in an airplane. She never had to.

From what I saw of the United States between Boston and St. Louis I concluded that it was too much built-up, starved for woods, open spaces, and country. I hope that it was not so conventionalized and conformist as it appeared from the air through the bemusing gaseous atmosphere. What an overcrowded, diminished, suffocating land, I thought. So much of this, I knew, had come about during my lifetime and, though unreasonably, I felt responsible.

The clouds I liked. I shall never have the same feeling about clouds again, for now I have known them, not face to face, but almost as equal to equal, as one knows woodland on the ground. We flew through no clouds that I noticed, but here and there a billowing cloud range loomed a bit higher than our plane, and I thought of the Chilmark hills at home, as seen from the road crossing the central Island plain. All these clouds were white, and this made them seem dependable. Other colors I have seen only from the ground.

I had viewed the Mississippi before, at New Orleans, and had once even steamed out of it on a freighter, but after I reached St. Louis I admired the river more and liked it better than before. It seemed still master in its own house, or in the wide expanse of its own continent. For mile after mile it was fringed with cottonwoods instead of condominiums, and there were only a few small craft instead of a glut of commerce.

I saw little of St. Louis, but judged it to be just another city. The choice among cities, or at least among the big, big cities, is pretty narrow today. But I'd rather go to St. Louis than to Chicago any old time.

Of course some things not on my list can be depended upon to be as much fun in this time of youth as they were

in mine. I am aware of that. Some may be more fun nowadays and may lead to a mellower nostalgia than my own.
But they are not so much fun for me at my age. There's no
going back.

Someone, of course, is sure to mention sex. It is impossible to leave sex alone, though with so much frankness
around and about, one doubts its genuine quality and sus-
pects adulteration.

My thought on the subject echoes Enid Bagnold who
wrote in her autobiography, "It's not till sex has died out
between a man and a woman that they can really love."
She went on:

> When I look back on the paint of sex, the love like a fox
> so ready to bite, the antagonism that sits like a twin beside
> love, and contrast it with affection, so deeply unrepeatable,
> of two people who have lived a life together (and one of
> whom must die) it's the affection that I find richer. It's
> what I would have again. Not all those doubtful rainbow
> colors. (But then she's old, one must say.)

Older, anyway, and not in all respects unlucky to be so.
When one has died, affection is the twin that outlives
mourning and restores a richness to life, and a quieter
awareness and self-knowledge to the heart.

∽

The great blue heron is almost always at the lagoon
when Graham and I walk to the Harbor Light in the morning. Yesterday the bird itself was hidden against the darkness of the outer beach, so what I saw was its reflection
winging across the tenderly lighted water. The heron has
a prehistoric manner of flight, and for a moment or two it
seemed not to be present at all, but a legend brought to
sight through the play of light and shadow.

I am always fascinated to see the great blue heron take flight, becoming slowly airborne with a flapping of wings, legs trailing, long neck and bill at first outstretched, then drawing back to the shoulders. A circling and soaring to attain height and speed, and then the great bird is away.

Blue really isn't the color. Thoreau, as usual, wrote the best description while he walked on a November afternoon beside the Assabet: ". . . a great slate-covered expanse of wing, suited to the shadows of the stream, a tempered blue as of the sky and dark water intermingled."

∽

All such matters are trivial in our civilization or in the values of the marketplace, and sometimes I feel that age is a time of triviality even when it has not reached the far bourn of dotage. At other times I am not so sure by half. Civilization, taken as a state of social compromise, a context of economics and world trade, or culture even, is a far from perfected science of living together on the earth. All involvement in it seems compromised by the temporal or Faustian.

One man's foot on the ground may, in a sense, be worth all of that. At least it is an affirmation and an example. If all must come to earth in the end, then this is as good as an ultimate, a fundamental short of death itself. Sooner or later one faces up to it.

George Borrow's colloquy between Jasper Petulengro, the gypsy, and himself, Lavengro, the scholar, was once famous, and I wonder how widely known it is in today's surge of new things. The gypsy speaks first:

"Life is sweet, brother."
"Do you think so?"
"Think so? There's night and day, brother, both sweet

things, sun, moon and stars, brother, all sweet things; there's likewise the wind on the heath. Life is very sweet, brother; who would wish to die?"

"I would wish to die."

"You talk like a gorgio — which is the same thing as talking like a fool — were you a Romany Chal you would talk wiser. Wish to die, indeed! A Romany Chal would wish to live forever!"

"In sickness, Jasper?"

"There's the sun and stars, brother."

"In blindness, Jasper?"

"There's the wind on the heath, brother. If I could only feel that, I would gladly live forever . . ."

I suppose that may be put down as book talk, and old-fashioned. But I doubt if in the most advanced similar colloquy of this current year, any party would refer to the day's stock market quotations, the G.N.P., or the consumer price index. The real fundaments don't change, even with different words found for them. When the mind turns toward childhood memories it turns at the same time to what always was, and if life is to persist, what must always be. Many people even wonder about the survival of a livable planet, a wonder that harks far back and looks far, though less far, ahead.

Living forever would be one thing, living for a long, long time is another. Euripides wrote: "Happy is he who has escaped the tempest-tossed sea and reached port. Happy is he who has got to the end of the labors of life." But also: "It is vain for old men to pray for death, to complain of age and the length of life, since if death came near, not one is willing to die; then old age is no longer burdensome to them."

This is pretty tricky. But the psychiatrist friend from whom I quoted before told me of the case of an old man bound incurably in hopeless suffering, who knew he must die, yet did not reach out for the release of the pills on the bedside table which would have ended everything. My psychiatrist friend believed that no one wishes to die. That is, there exists no will to death.

We think of such matters. There is nothing we do not at some time consider or contemplate, but today and its life remain. I walk out in the early morning with Graham and see the great blue heron and its reflection in the lagoon, and a sunrise flush in the sky. These and more else than I can describe inform me that I have come into a great fortune of years, and I mean to draw upon that account as long as I can.

More conservatively put is the opinion of Anacreon, who flourished in 376 B.C. (All the old Greeks seem to have flourished, and I don't think most contemporary Americans do. They are not sufficiently at home, and tend to make themselves less so. They are part of a flux. Give them a vacation and the chances are that they want to go "abroad," wherever that is.)

Anacreon's observation was this: "Old age is not, father, the heaviest of burdens, as thou thinkest; but whoever bears it unwisely, he is the party who makes it so; if he bears it without grumbling he sometimes in this way lulls it asleep, dexterously changing its character, taking away pain and substituting pleasure, but making it pain if he is peevish."

I have also come upon the merest fragment from the writings of Bion, who flourished about 280 B.C., and I bet he did. This single sentence appears in extracts from his works under the heading, "The Old":

"But the old man, smiling, shook his head and answered the boy."

At first I wished that I had more of this, and was tempted

to study Greek in order to look up the original. But then a better instinct prevailed, and I realized that the statement of Old Bion, as I suppose he was, is perfect as it stands. The rest is up to us.

YESTERDAY MORNING Graham and I started out in the darkness a little after six for a turn around the pond. We know that path as well as any path can be known, but I carried a flashlight because the way twists and narrows, there was ice on the uneven ground in some places, and no one ever knows where or when some fool or vandal may have introduced that too familiar thing in American life, an excavation. Americans are prone to excavate.

We had passed the dike, and I, in the lead, followed the succession of turns beyond until, rounding the most abrupt, I saw in the beam of the flashlight a better than medium-size skunk squarely in the path. We were approaching from its rear, which is no way to approach a skunk if you can make plans ahead of time. Skunks ought not to be abroad in January, but for two weeks the weather had been springlike even to that magical freshness in the morning and evening air. Any living creature would want to be outdoors early and late.

As between the skunk and myself I think the element of surprise was about equally divided. I shouted, intending, as much as intention was feasible at the time, to scare him into flight. Graham, whose reaction margin is also of the first order, shot past me at express-train speed toward the skunk, true to his habit of attack and pursuit, though most of it is only acting out an ancestral pattern, as he himself is aware. He laughs at himself sometimes over such sorties. In no time at all, he came charging back past me faster than before in the opposite direction, leaving a familiar sulphurous odor in the air.

It turned out that he had been only minimally affected, so that in another mile or so of walking, while the sun came up as the climax of a rosy-fingered dawn, and a breeze freshened still more, he had been aired out. Our good luck was due to the fact that Graham, even at high speeds, can turn on a dime, and the skunk was unable to plot a trajectory around the sharp bend in the trail. But the scene of the encounter was well marked.

One may meet a skunk at any time of his life, but one is best equipped who has matured in philosophy and love of nature. Thoreau deplored the extinction of nature's warriors in the environs of Concord, where he ranged afoot for ten miles in every direction to better advantage than most travelers who try to embrace the globe. He had known old men who had killed bears and moose in the country around beautiful Fairhaven Bay. By present-day standards I think the skunk is one of nature's warriors, if not among the tribal giants, and we should not hesitate to know him as a neighbor.

Thoreau often followed a skunk, and he knew how to do it. "Very slow," he wrote on a March day in 1854. "I hardly have to run to keep up with it. It has a long tail which it regularly erects when I come too near, and prepares to discharge its liquid." It runs, he wrote, "even when undisturbed, with a singular teeter or undulation, like the walking of a Chinese lady . . . There is something pathetic in such a sight, next to meeting one of the human aborigines of the country. I respect the skunk as a human being in a very humble sphere."

Instead of frightening that skunk where the path curves beyond the dike, Graham and I should have observed and followed it. I wonder, as Thoreau did, what the poor creature — poor by my standards but not necessarily by nature's — managed to find to eat during the winter. There must have been some unfrozen ground for our friend to probe in, and grubs not too deeply buried.

The encounter with the skunk, as modest an affair as it was, I cherish for its broader relevance.

In his newest book, *Beast or Angel*, René Dubos notes that the first cities came into being 5,000 years ago (but I say that Sheriff's Meadow is much older than that), and Babylon in the sixth century B.C. already had a population of some 200,000 inhabitants. I can't find what its population is today. What happened to Babylon?

Anyway, Mr. Dubos sees a historical process of urbanization which has not been accidental or contrived by political power. "It has resulted from the fact that city life has an appeal which, although commonly denied, seems nevertheless almost universal." He speaks of the "hope cities give of a life richer in unexpected experience, especially with regard to human contacts."

I don't want to enlist in any further campaigns of the war between country and village on the one hand, and city on the other, but I will assert my own preference and a conviction that it is widely shared, no matter what statistics may show. The daily feeling of homecoming that I find as an ultimate in the small and largely rural circle of my life is something different in quality from any corresponding experience the generality of city dwellers can know. The city offers a lodging overnight, so to speak, and the country offers home. Of course this will be disputed, because city people, being in the majority, can dispute anything with a fine prospect of success. The city and its excrescence, the suburb, will always win, population-wise — which is just the way to say it — but the hope of the unexpected, not especially in human relationships, which may not be all that important, seems to me to have better prospects in the country. It depends a great deal on what one wants to experience.

Graham and I wouldn't have asked to meet that skunk, but the unexpected meeting came off very well in the pre-twilight of a January morning.

∽

There is a good deal of talk about the energy crisis and of course we talk about it too. But other subjects are always coming up naturally. The other day someone started wondering how long ago the cannonballs in Memorial Park had been cemented together. They are ostentatiously cemented now into small pyramids beside the ancient cannon from which one is supposed to believe they might have been fired, though I don't quite see how. The equation of ballistics is too simple or too complicated for my mind — it's just that the big cannonballs don't look as if they could ever have gone through the muzzles of those sluggish relics of ancient artillery, tokens of giantism in their era as they were.

Originally, by which I mean the time when I first became aware of them, the cannonballs were piled loosely, in traditional readiness for another British invasion. The inevitable occurred some years later, not an invasion by the redcoats, but an exploit by boys who touched off charges of powder in the cannons by night. The sheriff, Tom Dexter, assigned himself to the case with zeal and indignation, but found it impossible to solve. His daughter-in-law, Alice, had supplied the boys with necessary accessories for the firing of the battery, and could have given evidence but didn't.

The cannonballs remained freely movable for some years more. I am sure of this, for one morning they were found scattered about the park. Report had it that they had been struck by lightning, a suggestion that I investigated in company with a member of the faculty of the University of Cincinnati. We concluded that lightning had not been involved, though there had been a coincidental heavy thunderstorm.

Shortly after this disturbing event the park commissioners had all the cannonballs cemented together in pyramids. I am not sure who was chairman of the park board, and therefore cannot fix the date. It may have been our friend Marshall Shepard who had a lifetime passion for neat conclusions. Betty and I wrote in his name one year when no candidate was listed, the office not being sought after, and our two votes elected him with a hundred per cent plurality.

This does not settle the question of when the cannonballs were painted with high gloss enamel, a point some of us have discussed this past day or so. The painting is one of the most obvious of facts. Those cannonballs glisten in sunshine, moonlight, and in rain, and they are a monument to peace not much second to ploughshares beaten out of swords. No other weaponry has been more conclusively removed from possible usefulness in combat.

We are no longer ready for another British invasion, but perhaps none will come. The first was a good while ago, and conditions have changed since. An expedition of Britishers marched in our Fourth of July parade a few summers back.

The subject of Memorial Park has been exhausted for the present, except for a question as to when it was that Enoch Cornell collected funds to erect the gray obelisk in memory of the G. A. R. veterans, of whom he was one. That must have been somewhere around the turn of the century. But one thing leads to another in the conversation of old men who have time for reflection and a curiosity to tie down uncertain memories.

When was it that the last sidewheeler came into Edgartown on schedule, or, for that matter, when was the last steamboat landing at what is now the town wharf? When did Jimmy Chadwick give up the coal business? When did Tony King Silva push a skiff out over the winter ice and rescue Ves Luce from peril? What year was the Harbor Light made automatic? Which of the hurricanes destroyed the old sail loft on the North Wharf?

Many weekly newspapers carried occasional departments of "Argument Settlers" for the purpose of answering such questions, but for every argument that was settled, another was born. Since I have become an old inhabitant I can understand that unresting examination into lost exactitudes of the past.

Yesterday someone was wanting to know when the selectmen had to send one of their number to insist that John Modley be interred in the West Side cemetery according to custom. Burial, the board thought, had been deferred long enough. As I came to know the story, Theodore Wimpenney, acting as chairman of the board of health, called at the Modley house, and there was John in his coffin standing up behind the sitting room door. To Mr. Wimpenney's protest, Mattie replied, "Why he's as sweet as a nut!" But I can't fix the date and I don't know anyone who can.

I do know that thirty-five years ago today nothing happened. The temperature stood at 6 above zero at 7:30 that morning. But the cold by that time had become a commonplace. The sun shone over a landscape covered in deep snow. I know this because I had decided to keep a journal, and I have a record to back me up.

It was the next day after town meeting that Ed Vincent told me about Joe Nose and Judge Dunham. Joe's nickname sprang from an obvious physical fact. He wanted to buy a piece of land from the North School lot to help out his property which was skimped on that side, but he didn't think he could get a vote through town meeting. Ed advised him to give Judge Dunham five dollars, relying on the judge's oratory to sway the meeting. The judge was a good talker. He gained the floor and reminded everyone what a worthy citizen Joe was, and how the town should let him have that little piece of land at a small price.

The next time Ed met Joe on the street he said, "Well, it worked out all right about your giving five dollars to Judge Dunham."

"Yes, Hed," said Joe, whose manner of speech was a bit odd, "only I didn't give him five dollars. I said to myself, 'If he'll talk for five, he'll talk for three,' so I gave him three dollars."

It may be that there is no one now living except myself who can give a true account of this. No wonder we cast our thoughts backward, we who can. For that matter, I am glad to have lived in the three-dollar era, even though my cup ran not over.

During most of my life such a thing as an economy of

abundance was unknown. For instance, you couldn't buy green vegetables in winter. Like all old persons, I regret nothing of what would now be privations, but take pride in what I lived through with satisfactions that are rare today. I ask what the western world has really gained in my lifetime, considering that the margin between an economy of abundance and an economy of scarcity becomes narrower each day.

⌒

I stood on a chair and sorted out a few more of the little books on the top shelf, this time at the right-hand side of the fireplace. Back at floor level I released my clutch on a forgotten copy of Sheridan's play *The Critic* and read it through again with greater interest because my brother and I saw a revival on Broadway many, many years ago. ("Many" is a modifier old people feel entitled to use twice-over. Just once is inadequate.)

I laughed immoderately at the performance, and I laughed again as I read the play. From the stage directions I could call up the action nicely. For instance:

> The two Nieces draw their daggers to strike Whisker-andos, the two Uncles at the instant, with their two swords drawn, catch their two Nieces' arms and turn the points of their swords to Whiskerandos who immediately draws two daggers and holds them to the two Nieces' bosoms.

Says Puff: "There's a situation for you! There's an heroic group! You see, the ladies can't stab Whiskerandos — he durst not strike them for fear of their uncles — the Uncles durst not kill him because of their Nieces — I have them all at a deadlock! — for every one of them is afraid to let go first."

"Why, then," says Sneer, "they must stand there for-ever!"

But Puff has a very fine contrivance, the sudden appearance of a Beefeater charging them all in the Queen's Name to drop their daggers or swords. I think it was Charles Townsend Copeland at Harvard who urged one of his students in a writing class to solve his problems of construction without calling on a Beefeater in the Queen's Name.

The advice was good, but other necessities now prevail. A time has come in literature when is it important to drop in a device or a symbol not to clear things up, but to prevent them from being clear.

For instance, in the John Fowles story *The Ebony Tower*, David's car runs over something "orange-brown, a mouse, but too big for a mouse, and oddly sinuous, almost like a snake, but too small for a snake." Out of curiosity David walked back and found "It was a weasel . . . Only the head had escaped. A tiny malevolent eye stared up . . ."

A reviewer wondered what the weasel was intended to mean. Later I read an interview with Fowles in which he said he had put the weasel in "afterward," but he didn't say how long afterward, or why. I can see why, though — the weasel was a modern equivalent of Sheridan's Beefeater in the Queen's Name, reversed of course. An author today who expects to hold up his head in public or especially at a cocktail party must have a conjuration to keep things from being understandable.

The *New York Sunday Times* defended Fowles — or apologized for him, I am not sure which — for employing ordinary narrative rather than the "new consciousness." Well, you can't have everything, can you? You may have to settle for a weasel, though on a temporary basis, for I can easily imagine a Charles Townsend Copeland of the future advising a damply inexperienced student to try to confuse his readers without calling on a run-over weasel with a tiny malevolent eye.

There are analogies among the arts, no matter what anyone says, and an instance is the phrase used by John Canaday to damn the painting of Thomas Hart Benton. Benton represented "reactionary narrative realism." What Canaday was really after was the craft of storytelling which runs through all the arts, even through music. I agree with Tom Benton who said that painting does not progress but only changes; and of course it changes back and forth, here today and gone tomorrow. But some things prevail forever in all the arts, and I doubt that storytelling will ever be laid finally at rest, even if you call it "reactionary narrative realism."

～

The great elm stumps in my front yard, though they were sawed off as close to the ground as possible, seem to have emerged starkly now that winter has come. The sodden grass has given way around them until they stand like monuments, or at least like massive pedestals for monuments. I'd like to use them for exactly that.

If I had enough money, I would commission two large and beautifully sensuous nude figures, going back to the Greeks for inspiration. This would not be a protest against the Puritan culture in which I was brought up, but rather a witness to an ideal from which, in my observation, the emancipated present departs. There are bare forms aplenty, but not enough fair attitudes. I see no obligation to a fugitive concept of "decency" but I think there should be one to beauty if the public is to be a sharer.

I would also rebuke all those who use the abbreviation "Ms.," not only because of their offense against the language but because of their backwardness on the subject of

sex. They seem not to realize that the sexes are dif-
ferentiated by nature rather than by prefixes, and to assume that a state of marriage makes any real difference in
modern society is to adopt an affectation of blindness.

But instead of my nudes I shall probably have a couple
of bird baths. This is a typically modern anticlimax.

Today at the very end of January I noticed a clump of
snowdrops blooming beside the mulberry tree at the front
gate. I feel just as cold now as I did before I noticed them.

Needing a fire last night, I sawed up a mulberry limb
that had been sacrificed long ago to give clearance to automobiles in the lane outside. The limb had been in the
cellar for a long time, and the sawed-up pieces burned
briskly with a dancing flame, so that nothing was left in
the morning but ashes. There were also the ashes of old
hopes, for the generation that planted this tree at my front
gate, as well as a number of others in town, had intended
to establish a silk industry on Martha's Vineyard. Silkworms wouldn't survive our winters, even though the sea
is a moderating influence, but this wasn't all. The mulberry tree chosen was not the right kind of mulberry for
silkworms. Our new entrepreneurs make mistakes as wide
and large but without leaving a legacy of magnificent
shade trees or anything as beneficent to their fellow men.

Tonight, looking for kindling in a hurry, I brought up
from the cellar the broken end of a thin plank and watched
it burn in the fireplace. It caught fire easily and from it
rose long green flames, licking into the draft of the
chimney. By this sign I knew that the fragment of plank
was from the sheathing of the last of the Noman's Land
boats to sail in and out of Edgartown.

Quickstep, Osmond Pease's boat, was broken up thirty or
forty years ago after he had given up the sea. It was
hauled to the field at the edge of Sheriff's Meadow near

the small house where Ozzie lived out his final years. After his death his niece gave us a good lot of copper-fastened pieces to burn for green flame on winter nights.

Betty was alive then, and she and I might have sat before the hearth as I did alone last night. But we hoarded the gift, and the occasion of what is hoarded is more often lost than not. With material things there is no great harm, but with life the stakes are higher. The remains of *Quickstep* were some of each.

∽

When I was a small boy I once stood in a darkened room where there was a dead baby. I had been sent by my mother with a note of condolence or perhaps with flowers from our yard, and I was shown upstairs in a house at the corner of Campbell and County Streets in New Bedford.

The baby's father was there, walking back and forth slowly in a darkening caused by the partly drawn curtains. He was Mr. Sullivan. The baby's coffin was under the windows at one side. I stood awkwardly while Mr. Sullivan took my mother's message, and then he asked me if I would like to see the baby. He made a slight directional gesture with one hand as he did so.

No, I didn't want to see a dead baby. As soon as I got outdoors again I started for home in a hurry. I suppose I was six or seven years old.

Another time way back then on Campbell Street there was an alarm of fire in the James E. Moore house next door to us on the west. The bells did not ring, for it was a "still" alarm. The fire, if there really was one, must have been of slight importance, for the firemen came trooping down the staircase almost at once singing, "The smoke went up the chimney just the same." They were merry firemen, but I learned later that all firemen sing this song under the same circumstances.

⌒

I learned today of Eugenia's death. She was one of Betty's oldest and best friends. Back in the early years of the Columbia School of Journalism she was devotedly reading and never seeming to finish Hardy's *The Mayor of Casterbridge*. Though so many of us own up to it reluctantly, the phrase "lifelong friendship" isn't much within anyone's natural experience. Most friendships turn out to be for a period only, for they are interrupted by separations, changes of age and interest, and perhaps most of all by antipathetic marriages. But, wonder of wonders, Betty's friendship with Eugenia skipped about from place to place and from year to year.

They were together at North Tisbury for a summer or two. Eugenia moved to Philadelphia, and we saw her there; she worked for the Curtis Publishing Company and like all except the major employees had to enter and leave by the back door, a fact that infuriated her uncle. She moved to Baltimore, where Betty stayed with her for many months. She moved again to Pittsburgh and we stopped off to see her when we visited Betty's old home in Uniontown. Once we saw her for a weekend in Washington; we had reunions in New York, and at last visited her at Seal Cove on Mount Desert Island.

Now, removed from all those years of association, and living alone with Graham, I learn that she is dead. The news comes in winter when the night is cold and there is ice in Sheriff's Meadow Pond. After the first resurgence of memories, I realize that what is past was already past. I would never have seen her again.

The keenest sadness I have now is that there is no one to

whom I can pass on the news of Eugenia's death. The word
has come and it must stop with me. Even with Graham, I
am more alone now than I was yesterday.

I shall end by being sorriest of all, not on account of
Eugenia, but on account of myself.

〜

Does anyone talk of the "compensations" of being
young? I don't think so, for youth is the springtime of
more than a single year. I suppose the compensations of
middle age are principally that although one has stopped
being young, one is nevertheless far from being old. In my
own middle years, during which a certain book gained
popularity, I was absorbed with curiosity as to whether life
really did begin at forty. I didn't think it possible, but the
idea, once absurd, had become encouraging.

Now my life begins in summer at five o'clock in the
morning, and in winter more likely at six or even six-
thirty, and there are compensations for the everyday,
familiar fact of aging. I have never seen them stated con-
vincingly, though, and wonder if they can be.

A while ago the American Medical Association took
what I suppose should have been my side of a debate.
"People over sixty-five," said the A.M.A., "should not be
regarded as a group with uniform characteristics and problems. Rather, they should be regarded as millions of individuals with countless variations and combinations —
physical, mental, emotional, social and financial."

Right away it occurred to me that the A.M.A. was thinking more of itself and its members than of old people.
There's no dodging the fact that when people get old, they
have old age in common and do not want to be deprived of
the distinction. Only the middle-aged are careless or sensi-

tive about their years. And I don't want the A.M.A. depriving me of my compensations.

Only the old can say with a final indisputable pride, "I have survived," and sometimes even add, "So far, so good." If this is not a compensation of age, what is it?

When one is asked "How ya doing?" no reply is expected, but the older question "How are you?" is also usual. There is valor as well as pig-headedness in the assurance so often given, "I never felt better in my life." Even to be able to answer the inquiry is something.

He who speaks out so bravely, as stating his position against age, is likely in the next hour or so to meet a friend of the same number of years who looks as if he had been dug up from under a chicken house — so perhaps the first old man was telling part of the truth, anyway.

No matter what claim he asserts, he won't escape the admonition of doctor, wife, or friend, "You've got to slow down. You can't expect to do what you did twenty years ago." Or thirty or forty years ago. But of course that is what any determined old person, or old fool, wants to do and will try to do unless prevented.

The A.M.A. changed the name of its Committee on Geriatrics to Committee on Aging, a rare instance of retreat from elegance or pretension to plain speech. I suppose the A.M.A. was outflanked by the patent medicine people who, so far as the general public was concerned, might as well have invented geriatrics.

The best witness against the A.M.A. generalization would be Old Man Minick in Edna Ferber's story of long ago, who fled the well-meant regimentation of a proper family household for the more congenial companionship of an old men's home. The fact of all being in the same boat at the latter end of life is a fact of ultimate jurisdiction.

Let's face it, too: old people no longer have responsibility for the future of civilization, if civilization has a future.

~

Our Council on Aging offers the solace of books, magazines, games, and a piano. Coffee, tea, and lemonade are appropriately served. As to lemonade, most old people can say, "This is where I came in," remembering the adventure that making lemonade used to be. The second time around may be better, on the whole.

The Council maintains a schedule of weekly activities which has included ceramics instruction, bridge, ladies' swimming, and luncheon served by the culinary arts department of the Regional High School. The Council offers free transportation to and from church services and for other purposes, even if what the aging want to do at the moment is to hitch a ride.

All this is a change from treatment of the aging in former times. One old man, soon after the turn of the century, having shoveled the snow from the sidewalk at the Four Corners in order to earn a dollar or two, and wishing to earn a bit more, was told to shovel the snow back again. He went away with whatever was due him, without even his pride intact. And Alonzo D. Vincent, a veteran of the Grand Army of the Republic, ignored most of the year and referred to, if at all, as Lonnie D., received special privileges on Memorial Day.

"I got a ride to Oak Bluffs and back," he said to me, "and it didn't cost me nothing."

The Council also arranges bus tours, autumn foliage tours, and trips to places with names that suggest they may be fleshpots. Even if this last turns out to be illusion, it is good for aging morale. I believe the state Department of Elder Affairs has something to do with all this, and references are made to the Senior Citizens Charter that emerged from a White House Conference on Aging in 1961. After the conference was over, the smoke went up the chimney just the same.

They can keep their charter, but I am in favor of our Center after being assured that it does not offer supervised play. That life might begin and end with supervised play seemed intolerable. Supervised play is an urban concept that got out of hand.

Just now I've read that elderly people are aiming for what is called "dynamic maturity." I doubt if they are aiming for anything of the sort. They know very well where the sun stands in the sky. Maturity took place when the apple was ripe and the fireflies flitted in the orchard. Best keep away from the apple tree at this autumnal season. Time has run out for that word "dynamic" too. If one has to use it, there's something funny and undynamic going on behind the pretentious front.

Old people don't like to be told what to do or what to think. Not as a rule. They've generally had enough of that in their lives. They don't expect to skip rope. Some can swim and dive and some can walk the legs off younger generations, but the bench under the plane tree at the edge of the courthouse lawn is well placed. The sitting there is good at almost all seasons.

"Stand out from between me and the sun," Diogenes is supposed to have said to young Alexander of Macedon.

❧

When grapes in the market are priced low enough I like to buy a package and tie some of them in the rosa multiflora bush outside my kitchen window. The mockingbird, a winter visitor who has eaten the last of the rose hips, does not find it strange that the bush has suddenly begun bearing grapes. Of course other birds are attracted also.

Occasionally I take grapes to Coco, Edith Blake's African gray parrot, whose friendship I have succeeded in cultivating, though still within strict bounds.

The other night I left a pretty good lot of store-bought grapes on top of the kitchen range, and in the morning all were gone except for a few fragments mixed with stems. I could not imagine what marauder could have been responsible, for there was no sign of mice.

I mentioned the mystery to Edie Blake, who said without hesitation, "Graham!" She added, "He likes fruit."

Yes, he does like fruit, but I am disappointed if it really was he who broke our understanding and helped himself.

⌒

Anyone who has lived as long as I must have seen eras come to an end. This is the likelier because eras are held so cheaply nowadays. Most people, especially journalists, would as soon open or close an era as not, and scientific discoveries, wars, space shots, and so on are natural punctuations for world eras.

There are also quieter, personal ones that stand even more sharply apart, and for Betty and me one came to an end when Hallowell's Restaurant on lower Main Street began serving liquor after the repeal of prohibition. This sounds like the beginning of an era rather than the end, but it wasn't. It was the end.

The Hallowells opened their restaurant roughly with the onset of the Depression, as ill-starred a time as there could have been. They criticized some of the carpenter work that was done preparatory to the opening, and the contractor replied, "It'll last as long as you're likely to be here." But, surprisingly, their business took hold at once, and grew and grew until it represented the town's only real prosperity.

It was warm and comfortable and inexpensive. The fishermen liked to gather there. Mrs. Hallowell did the cooking with rare competence and appeal, and of course there was no tipping of the one waitress or at the counter on the lunchroom side of the establishment.

For several years Betty and I ate a meal there once on almost every day, including turkey on Thanksgiving and salmon and peas on the Fourth of July. Mostly we had fish chowder or beef stew at twenty-five cents a steaming bowlful, and for another nickel we could finish off with a wedge of Mrs. Hallowell's cream of banana pie with its towering meringue. Mrs. Hallowell had potted plants in the window and the quality of the restaurant was helped out by a dog named Lady and a canary in a cage. You might live a long lifetime and never know a restaurant like Hallowell's.

Occasionally we had a steak, but not often, because it cost seventy-five cents which was as much as you could spend at Hallowell's unless you ordered both steak and a banana split. The steak was not the tenderest, but the banana split was gorgeous. In spring the hardy seamen of the big yawl *Manxman* ate at Hallowell's while the vessel was being fitted for the new season, and they always had banana splits because they were hungry and on expense accounts.

Sid Gordon, who called himself "the plastered plasterer," ate at Hallowell's, and so did Tom Baylies, Willie Bell, who had a gift of words, Marshall Shepard of the park commission, Red Ward, and Joe Two-Tail, who was so known because he once told of having seen a rat with two tails.

Across the street from the restaurant was George Knight's antique shop where, in summer, cronies gathered at the noon hour, sitting among the whale ivory, old posters, chairs, bureaus, and odds and ends, talking about the sea, or the Townsend Plan, or the W.P.A. The door was always open, and there was a sort of contrapuntal effect with Hallowell's.

Meantime great events took place. Franklin D. Roosevelt was elected to the presidency in 1932, and in December 1933 the Noble Experiment of Prohibition came to an end with the ratification of the amendment by Utah.

Mr. Hallowell announced that he would apply for a license and sell liquor.

"If I don't do it someone else will," he said.

About this same time Bunny Norton, a little old man, was asked why he mowed the grass in back of his barn. He replied, "Because if I don't do it, nobody else will." The estrangement between these two statements deserves to be memorialized.

Of course there was no doubt that someone would sell liquor, but Mrs. Hallowell, adamant in W.C.T.U. principles, did not believe it should be her husband. As for herself, she didn't want any liquor around the place. The ensuing family argument spilled over into town awareness and into town talk, and it was possible to tell how things were going by the number and length of the contusions on Mr. Hallowell's face.

Mr. Hallowell prevailed so far as getting the license went, but Mrs. Hallowell kept a tactical advantage by smashing bottles of whiskey and gin on the rocks behind the restaurant. The disagreement continued actively until Mr. Hallowell sold control of the place, bought a washing machine for his wife, and told her to stay home.

So Hallowell's broke up, sort of, and for Betty and me an era came to an end. There it stood, historic and apart, with a fixed character that eras ought to have. Things would never be the same on lower Main Street, though a successor restaurant was to grow to a different prosperity. Nor would Betty and I ever be so young again.

That the Depression thinned out a little at the same time was no more than a coincidence. For us it was a minor one.

Another and quite different era, recent as some memories go, wasn't private but was privately noticed by us. It followed the close of World War II, though the war had nothing to do with it. The dying off of the older generation in our town would have occurred anyway, mortality being what it is.

Older generations are passing all the time, but what disappeared now and forever was the Establishment which had carried over from the nineteenth into the twentieth century. Time was chopped off and long roots were severed. So few now could look back before 1900 with their own eyes, and these few with small chance of sharing what they saw, and what they knew.

An unprecedented transition period had slipped into the past during which automobiles had replaced horses, bathrooms had replaced privies, and cardboard cartons seemed to have replaced cows. The unexpected multiplicity of new things now seemed natural, and those to whom they seemed natural were strangers to the departed generations which looked upon them with feelings hard to separate out.

Chester Pease's livery stable inherited from his father was long gone, and during the later years of his life he had sold cars. He said he ought to have put in a bathroom twenty years before he did, but he and his kind didn't jump at new things. Now he and Mattie had observed their golden wedding and both were gone with the ripe companions of their time.

But it wasn't youth that had come into control — not yet. Middle was the age whose day had so suddenly and inevitably arrived. The new Middle Age, though, was a singular one, in some part more or less of the period of adult infantilism which observers had so much to say about and to write about during the period between the two world wars.

What we noticed was the almost complete change in the roles of leading town figures — no longer the skepticism as to progress, no more the strongly asserted individual opinions in the vein we had known, no more the superstitions and familiar doubts. We could see clearly that an era had ended and that a new one was begun. Some may dispute me, but in this free country one is entitled to pick out era endings and beginnings as he sees them with his own eyes.

◇

An end of one era important in world civilization I have seen indisputably, experiencing it close at hand, and no one can refuse to acknowledge its pivotal character. The ancient craft of printing reached the evening of its long day while I looked on and saw the lights go out. The *Vineyard Gazette*, in common with almost all newspapers great and small, "went offset." No more the types set by hand, no more the Linotype of Mergenthaler casting line after line from hot metal, the completeness of the revolution proved by the fact that Linotypes were no longer manufactured in the United States. And this was the machine that had set modern printing and publishing on its way to speed and greatness.

Only a little while ago the succession from old masters and practitioners remained intact. Our own Old Editor, had he been alive, would still have said to his daughter on Friday morning, "Hand me some nonpareil slugs, will you, Elizabeth."

Nonpareil slugs — where are they now? Gone with the old names, some for good, some to be adapted to the new style of photographic composition — Bodoni, Caslon, Caxton, Elzevir, Goudy. Gone the apprentice boys with their rollers called breyers; the finish rules, three-em dashes, chases, mallet, and planer; what Eugene Field wrote about the printing office towel; the old type sizes — elite, minion, brevier, great primer. Ed Howe in Atchison, Kansas, and William Allen White in Emporia. For that matter, Bennett, Raymond, Greeley, Ochs, Pulitzer, Hearst in New York and elsewhere. Change everywhere.

I thought of Carlyle in *Sartor Resartus*, remembering him well enough to look him up: "He who first shortened the labor of copyists by the device of movable types was disbanding hired armies, and cashiering most kings and senates, and creating a whole new democratic world: he had invented the art of printing."

No types are cast or set now. A keyboard machine punches a tape with significant little holes, the tape runs through a computer which produces an image to be quickly processed photographically into readable copy. I asked the man why the computer kept stopping and starting, and he said this was because its memory was short. It had to reflect a little before it could continue.

Strange to any old printer was the spectacle of young men and girls cutting up the paper images of what once would have been type, fitting them into complete pages with pictures here and there, so that the pages could be photographed and turned into plates. Not the printing surfaces familiar in letterpress now, but these thin sheets of metal sensitized to choose between water and ink; and printed not from the sheets themselves but from a fast-revolving blanket on a cylinder of the press. All a fantasy to me, but real. The new day of printing.

"Time out of mind" — familiar phrase and true scale of an important value. I don't know who said it first, but there's also "time in mind," I suppose, looking backward and forward, important to me at my age as long ago when I went to school.

I am indebted to Random House for definitions, though any recent dictionary would do as well. *Offset:* "a process in which a lithographic stone or metal or paper is used to make an inked impression on a rubber blanket which transfers it to the paper being printed, instead of being made directly on the paper." *Letterpress:* "matter printed by letters or type in relief rather than intaglio or planographically." But I'm no clearer now.

It was the typographical unions that brought all this about, not in small shops like ours, but in the great urban centers where costs were so increased — all the more by unnecessary resetting of material once set already and therefore available in type or plate or matrix form — that only a revolution in technology could meet the pressure. Railroading had the term "featherbedding" and publishing used the word "bogus"; in both cases the meaning was the same. I think this was a sad way for Gutenberg and Mergenthaler to have died.

Strong arms broke up the old Duplex press with sledges and bars — but I was still thinking of it as a new press. They cut its main shaft of steel with an acetylene torch and dragged out the heavy parts with a winch in a truck and took them away for junk. They dangled our still functional Linotype with all its delicate parts from a crane, and it swung in the air like humanity lynched.

I looked on for a while, and then Graham and I walked home in what happened to be a lowering twilight. I could see the two of us as if I were an onlooker at a movie, and we receded in time and distance like the fade-out of an old silent film. There should have been rain and a shining pavement, and someone singing in the distance, but we were in nature, not in art. Though I wonder if there was a sharp dividing line, really. We had left an era behind.

WHEN GRAHAM WAS A PUPPY he was a handful of softness. I could lift him easily with one hand and the force of gravity hardly fought back. I looked up from a book in the living room one morning and saw him waddling toward me with a purposeful gait. It required some doing, but this mite of a dog rose up, shoved my book to one side, and put his forefeet in my lap. I took this as a thoughtful gesture on his part, and wanted to return the affection. My hubris was inexcusable, for I had known many dogs of many ways, but all of them encouraged a good deal of hubris in their masters, if only to make their masters comic characters later on.

In my gratification I put the book wholly aside and made Graham welcome, assuring him that he was a fine dog and esteemed by me. This assurance did not interest him much.

Not until the scene had been repeated a few times did I realize that Graham was not giving me complimentary attention but was asking for something.

His petitions usually fell under one of three heads: (1) he wanted to go out; (2) he wanted to go out and had no intention of going unless I would go with him; (3) he wanted something to eat. Communication between us was improved but not perfected. In the end it was I rather than Graham who did the learning. How do you teach something to a puppy who has already worked things out in a satisfactory way for himself and is only waiting for you to catch on?

Graham grew older and much larger. Everyone now regards him as a very large collie, though he is well within the breed limits and almost an inch less in height than one predecessor, Dundee Bold. The odds are all on his side when he strides into a room and puts his front legs into my lap. He does not exactly tower over me, but he subordinates me. His eyes are above my eye level. He could look down on me but he doesn't; his attention, his inattention really, is directed elsewhere. He is patient. He can afford to wait. No one can be as ostentatiously ignored as I am by Graham at these times, except that he holds me powerless under his unconcern.

Yet it is he who is making a request. Good God, I say to myself sometimes, what a ghostly way to ask for something! If I repeat such a thought to Graham he does not even glance at me. He might be attending to some distant preoccupation of his own, but I suspect that all his faculties are relaxed and at rest.

Before he makes one of his requests he finds it expedient to wait until I am comfortably settled down. He knows I am most vulnerable when I am trying to read a book. I got through a novel of Anthony Trollope last winter in spite of him, but not without a good many lost interludes. He gives no sign of dissatisfaction and may even seem to be asleep, but the moment I have relaxed in my chair, up he rises and with a preliminary stretch forward and back, advances upon me.

I do have some measures of defense. I may contrive to put a table in front of me, an open door on one side, and a sofa on the other. In this situation Graham simply puts his forepaws on the couch, resembling the King of Beasts rather more than an ordinary collie. He's still impossible to ignore.

Sometimes, sensing obduracy on my part, he will rear upon a chair on the opposite side of the room. The distance does not weaken his purpose. Can I refrain from glancing in his direction? Not possibly. I know he's putting on an act, but it's a pretty good act, and his inattention persists in being compelling.

It might be embarrassing, I think, if a visitor should come into the room and find me sitting on one side of the room, and Graham on the other side, head erect, front paws up, in a trained animal act reminiscent of Karl Hagenbeck. I mean embarrassing to me. I would feel subordinated or maybe ignominious.

The only possible solution for me is based upon a canon repeated to me a number of times by Henry Volkening, good friend and wisest of counselors: "When all else fails, give up."

Anyway, what Graham wants is usually what I really want. If the sun is shining, spring, summer, or fall, I am pleased to be treading one of our old paths around Sheriff's Meadow Pond while Graham makes sorties and investigations. Or to be bound for the Island's north shore, the woods and the native outdoors. In winter the situation is not much different, though Graham, being better equipped than I against cold weather, sometimes makes it a stiff choice for me to agree with him.

Some think the planet will die so far as man is concerned by the year 2000, done to death by man himself. A lot of people disagree, especially those whose life span may extend beyond the year 2000, and who therefore have a conflict of interest. I made one turn of centuries and cannot make another, and therefore I am without the shadow of a conflict of interest in the matter, and see no possibility that the planet can be saved. The hour is already much too late.

The more, then, that I should join Graham in search of the natural satisfactions that mean so much to us both. How much margin remains to me is not worth a guess, but I should make the most of it, and if Graham assists to this end I am in his debt.

⌣

If in February Graham's requests seem unreasonable, that is my way of looking at things, not his. There is no way of getting rid of February except by living through it on whatever terms it offers. Would we spare it from our lives if we could? I think not. We of coastal New England like our bitter medicine not in spite of, but because of, its bitterness.

In Sparta the newborn were washed in icy streams or exposed on winter hillsides to test their capacity for Spartan survival. In the New England to which I was born we have a somewhat lesser test, known as February, though we clothe our infants as well as ourselves against it, perhaps as much for reasons of morality as for any other. Little boys and little girls are not supposed to know what their nakednesses are like, though the secret is not well kept nowadays. In February it is better kept than in most other months.

Freezing is a drying process, and therefore I hung my underwear and bath towels on the line as usual, watching them freeze and dance their stiff modern jigs. But when I took this boardlike laundry into the house again and allowed it to melt, it seemed as wet as at the beginning.

A night or two before the end of the month Graham and I made our circuit in the soft light of a full moon. It had not risen high enough to cast an image into the pond, but the next night we saw it far aloft and the moonglade across the water surpassed in loveliness any I had ever seen. So keep coming the new experiences, or the sense of them, no matter how old you are. The ripple of light across the pond came toward us in a broad, glistening track, and we slowed our pace, relishing as well the sharp clear air and our inner stir of blood to which I could put the proper name — vitality. That the essential pleasure was Graham's as well as my own was one of the surest things I knew.

On our walk after breakfast the next morning we saw the moon again, appearing just as full, in the eastern sky, and a quite different glade across the pond. We reached the lighthouse and, looking back toward the town, watched another glade, this time in the tranquil, darkened harbor. Then appeared the first red-gold flush of morning, but we did not wait to see it spread.

Often the moon itself appears alone in Sheriff's Meadow Pond, floating as if it had been dropped in and lost.

February we lasted out, and March too, until on the next to the last day came Easter. After breakfast Graham and I walked to our own sunrise service at the lighthouse, but we were too late. No matter, rain was soaking the causeway, the sky lowered, and we had seen Christ risen as each best can in his own way.

Later on Easter someone asked, "Was there a minister at your sunrise service?" I said, "No," and added a few words

about the sky and the rain. Another person, listening, remarked, "Oh, one of those!" — meaning that I was one of
the modern tribe who beg off from God and true religion
with soft talk about nature. Well enough. He had me
typed accurately according to his own views.

But Paul Tillich wrote: "Religion — at least in some of
its recent interpreters — is a whole of symbols in which our
relation to the ground and meaning of existence is expressed. Being religious is being ultimately concerned —
and this the intellectual of our days is, even if he expresses
his ultimate concern in negative terms. Religion is not a
collection of theoretical statements of a questionable or
absurd or superstitious character. Such a religion could not
be accepted by any intellectual who is not willing to
sacrifice his intellectual honesty."

Leaving aside my dubious claim to being a respectably
qualified intellectual, I wonder whether Tillich has caught
us all in his net of wide mesh, or whether he has really ex-
cused us to go our own way in reason, walking on whatever
side of the street we choose, or in the middle. If we consider
ourselves caught, we are positively religious; if we are ex-
cused, we are negatively religious but religious all the same
without recourse.

It is all one to me, for my satisfaction now is just to await
the event.

∽

Our winter housekeeping, Graham's and mine, went
pretty well. I continued now and then to make chicken
chowders or lamb stews, and I could also cook a chicken,
browning it on the top of the stove in a skillet, and finishing
it in the oven. I usually worried about it, but it came out
all right. I could also make one special chicken casserole,
using sherry and Parmesan cheese.

I have not yet learned how to open a loaf of bread properly. At one end the waxed paper seems to have been heat-treated into a tight seal which does not easily come apart. At the other end is the maker's label which looks as if it would be coaxed off, but of course it can't be. No matter what procedure I try, the wrapper is mutilated. I don't care particularly except that I feel I should be bright enough to open a loaf of bread.

Almost all packaged goods come with printed instructions. You are told to slip your thumb under the edge and lift gently, also to close tab to preserve freshness. The other day a label invited me to pull a red tape to open, but there was no red tape, only a red line where I assume a tape should have been.

I should like to go back to the age of my early memories when most things came in barrels. Puffed Rice was scooped out of barrels at Braley's grocery store when it first came on the market in New Bedford, but Shredded Wheat and Grape Nuts in my time were always packaged.

〰

One night just before our bedtime Graham and I went out into the thickness of a new fog around Sheriff's Meadow Pond. Notwithstanding the fog, the moon glowed through — and "glowed" is the descriptive word. The fog shifted in a light breeze but the moonlight remained constant with an eerie effect. I wondered if it was like that when young Pip went into the marshes in *Great Expectations*, and the gates, dikes, and banks came bursting at him through the mist. Familiar objects in unexpected likenesses burst through at Graham and me, misted but dimly glowing.

Earlier in the day I had seen two great blue herons at the pond, and I supposed they were sleeping in the fog-bound pines or rushes on the far side from the path.

So many memorable things. With the arrival of April
two snowy egrets, a quawk, and a great blue heron in John
Butler's Mud Hole. Enough for the first expected pageantry of the new spring.

⌒

The two sayings that best characterized the everyday
culture of my youth were "If you don't like it you can lump
it" and "You can put it in your eye and see clear."

H. L. Mencken's dictionary of quotations classifies the
"lump it" saying as American, and says it is not of record
before the nineteenth century. I suppose it must have been
American, but we of New England always thought of it as
our own. Mencken says that "lump" meant "endure," but
it never did where I was brought up. I suppose it could be
interpreted as "to put up with" but much more clearly it
meant to choke down, gulp, swallow, or stomach as best one
could.

"Put it in your eye and see clear" hardly needs any con-
struing, but for us it implied a scathing note of defiance.
What, after all, could you put in your eye and see as clearly
as before? Only the thing of least consequence that someone had described or proposed, and to which you wish to
administer the utmost in belittlement. The rebuke usually
took better than an average vaccination.

Most aphorisms were obscure to me in my boyhood. One
of the most obscure was the one about nettles not hurting
you if you grasped them firmly. I had never seen a nettle,
at least anything known by that name, but I knew about
briars, and grasping them was no good.

And there was the bit about the idle magnet, put away
safely in a drawer and its magnetism gone when finally it
was taken out. It never occurred to me that a magnet's

idleness could have any relation to me. I detested that priggish admonition, "When duty whispers low, *Thou must,*/The youth replies, *I can.*" Even at the age of nine in the Mary B. White School I could see through this. How did the youth know whether he could or not?

Just as much of a put-on was Bulwer-Lytton's "In the lexicon of youth, which fate reserves/for a bright manhood, there is no such word/as — *fail.*" No logic here, I thought; no sense whatever.

So many foolish sayings, even "I can't complain." A person who can't complain, and with cause, is in a bad way.

◇

While shaving the other morning I nicked my chin as occasionally I do, notwithstanding the difficulty of doing so with the latest in safety razors. To stop the bleeding, I applied a small piece of toilet paper, making sure that it was well stuck and would serve its purpose until after breakfast.

I set out on my morning walk with Graham in all innocence, and evidently the scrap of tissue was still in place when we reached home after our three miles. I kept an appointment at the garage at nine o'clock, and it occurred to me that the mechanics and bystanders were looking at me curiously. That wasn't remarkable, though, and Graham and I walked home through the busy morning streets.

I worked at my typewriter until mailtime, say ten-thirty or eleven, then walked to the post office and back. The usual loiterers and passers-by greeted me. I chatted briefly with a neighbor, worked a while longer, and washed up for lunch. Looking in the mirror then, I was chagrined to see that torn patch of toilet paper still adhering to my chin. Ruefully I took it off.

The embarrassment of having been abroad with this homely device so conspicuous was not serious enough to last long, but I minded having exposed myself as an absent-minded member of the tribe of old men. If we don't stick together and keep our standards up, where are we?

Old men tend to be slack about their shoelaces. They tend to wear socks of different colors and to forget to button their pants. They put on some of their clothing inside-out. They are tolerant of egg and coffee stains on their shirts or jackets.

Thoreau, who did not live to be old, wrote: "How earthly old people become — mouldy as the grave . . . They remind me of earth-worms."

And Emerson at the age of thirty-eight: "Nature abhors the old, and old age seems the only disease; all the others run into this one."

So much we have to contend with, with how much hope of overcoming? Best take what care we can.

There is also the matter of incontinence. The word has a certain austerity but the fact it describes is inelegant beyond any other weakness of mankind.

I knew a brisk little man in his middle or late seventies, the very fashion plate of a retired man-of-the-world, just sporty enough in his tweed jacket and slacks, ready with anecdotes of far travel and books, admired by the ladies for his wit and his white eyebrows contrasting with an all-season tan. His mustache turned up properly at the ends, and his eyes were blue. There was only one trouble with him. He leaked a little.

His custom was to call at the house of a neighbor next door to watch her color television set when certain programs were on. After he departed, the household staff noticed that the seat of the chair he had occupied was conspicuously damp. Or wet.

This was not a circumstance that should be mentioned, but in the way of small town and neighborhood talk it was mentioned. It was brought up especially in relation to other cases of the kind, for instance that of a retired professor who had held an important chair at a big university and who, in his later years, wet the bed a little, to put it mildly, and expected his landlady to take no more notice of this than of a spider's web in the corner.

Who knows what and where dotage is? It has boundaries as fluidly and flexibly defined as those of the Sargasso Sea, which is bounded on all sides by water. Younger people do not understand how their elders, beyond a certain age, can become so accustomed to the smell of urine that they go about unaware. I know I don't wholly understand it myself.

The young, though, had best be as understanding as they can. Emerson at the age of thirty-eight could pass judgment on all old people, but he himself lost his better faculties long before he died at seventy-nine. Publishers here and abroad urged him to hurry up with a volume of hitherto uncollected writings, but there was no more hurry in him. His old friend, J. E. Cabot, wrote later, "Mr. Emerson applied himself to the task, though with a heavy heart, partly from being forced into an enterprise which he had not intended, but still more perhaps from a sense of inability, more real than he knew, which was beginning to manifest itself.

"He made, accordingly, but slow progress," Mr. Cabot went on, "so that in the summer of 1872 he had got ready little more than the first piece, Poetry and Imagination, the proof-sheets of which were in his hands — indeed had for some time been in his hands — when on the 24th of June his house was burned down and all possibility of work put an end to for the time . . . The proof-sheets showed that already before the accident his loss of memory and mental grasp had gone so far as to make it unlikely that he would in any case have been able to accomplish what he had undertaken. Sentences, even whole pages, were repeated, and there was a confusion of order beyond what even he would have tolerated . . ."

And Emerson, who at thirty-eight had observed nature abhorring the old, still had seven years to go. A little bed-wetting for an old professor still immersed in research may be minor in the overall scale of life. It can be a nuisance, though.

∽

Two words that overawed me in youth were "gainsay" and "vouchsafe." I would gladly have used them if I had dared, but both courage and occasion were lacking. Finally I thought that if I waited long enough they would go away. I was right. They have gone away.

∽

Walking down Main Street the other day, Graham and I came to an automobile standing beside the curb abreast of the drugstore. No one was in the automobile, its engine was not running, and it wasn't going anywhere. It was just standing still. But its warning light insistently signaled a left turn.

Here, I thought, and mentioned to Graham, was a perfect symbol of the age of communication — just pure communication. Something was being said, because somebody had pushed a button or turned a switch, and what was being said was not in any language because a vocabulary wasn't needed. The rote of our times was sufficient, and you could pay attention or not, as you wished. Nobody was paying attention, but communication went right on just the same.

⌒

I have come to the subject of meditation on our morning walks again, though meditation in a special sense, like that of the sentry in *Iolanthe*. I sometimes think of things that astonish *me*, whether or not they would astonish *you*. When we arrive home I may not have exercised my brains at all, but they have beckoned me on into territory I had never planned to enter.

James Harvey Robinson explains the action plan of how this sort of thing happens: "The first thing we notice is that our thought moves with such incredible rapidity that it is almost impossible to arrest any specimen of it long enough to have a look at it. When we are offered a penny for our thoughts, we always find that we have recently had so many things in mind that we can easily make a selection which will not compromise us too nakedly. On inspection we shall find that if we are not downright ashamed of a great part of our spontaneous thinking, it is far too personal, ignoble, or trivial to permit us to reveal more than a small part of it. I believe this must be true of everyone."

Perhaps it would be more true of the elderly than of others, for their minds wander. But their minds also empty out quickly and automatically, and their worst confession may well be that of being empty-headed at a given moment. Though the effort is frustrating, they may be lucky in a failure to recall whatever it was they were thinking about. Their minds seem to specialize in things just beyond reach.

On my walks with Graham I go through a lot of thoughts as well as through a lot of scenery, and usually it is with the thoughts as it was with my observation of Alida Gulick's lights when we passed by at six this morning. I must have noticed whether they were on or off, but I can't remember.

Sometimes, though, a sort of theme opens ahead just as the dike path does, and I follow it until I reach home, and even later. I will provide an instance. After we had crossed the dike this morning I found myself fancying a resemblance between Ernest Hemingway and George Borrow.

My father was a Borrovian, which means that he read and admired the books of George Borrow, 1803–1881, "English traveler, philologist and writer, noted for his works on gypsies." One critic wrote of him long ago: "I am convinced that he could not help dealing with himself as a hero . . . It was impossible for him to let slip an occasion to tell of his feats of walking, riding, fighting and speaking."

Is this like Hemingway, so far, or isn't it? A biographical dictionary says Borrow "tramped through England, met gypsies and a road girl celebrated as Isopel Berners." He met her in the leafiness of Mumper's Dingle, and the fact that she was no Hemingway kind of heroine may bring up again the suggestion that Hemingway had no heroines. Catherine in *A Farewell to Arms* is characterized by her nothingness, in the expressive phrase of Otto Friedrich, who reconsidered Hemingway in *The American Scholar*. She was, he said, an unreal creation and one of Hemingway's most typical.

Isopel Berners is different. Borrow, the Romany Rye or gypsy gentleman, has sought seclusion in Mumper's Dingle with the horse and tinker's outfit acquired from one Slingsby. Here, then, come the ruffianly Flaming Tinman, otherwise Blazing Boswell, with his moll and the road girl, spoken to as Belle. The descent into the dingle is precipitous, and the Flaming Tinman has some difficulty with his horse.

When, however, he had reached the bottom of the descent, he turned his head, and perceiving me, as I stood bareheaded, without either coat or waistcoat, about two yards from him, he gave a sudden start, so violent that the backward motion of his hand had nearly flung the horse upon his haunches . . .

"You need not be afraid," said I, addressing myself to the man, "I mean you no harm; I am a wanderer like yourself — come here to seek for shelter — you need not be afraid; I am a Romany chabo by matriculation — one of the right sort, and no mistake . . ."

Dashing past the other horse and cart, which by this time had reached the bottom of the pass, appeared an exceedingly tall woman, or rather girl, for she could scarcely have been above eighteen; she was dressed in a tight bodice and a blue stuff gown; hat, bonnet or cap wore she none, and her hair, which was flaxen, hung down on her shoulders unconfined; her complexion was fair, and her features handsome, with a determined but open expression. She was followed by another female, about forty, stout and vulgar-looking, at whom I scarcely glanced, my whole attention being absorbed by the tall girl.

"What's the matter, Jack?" said the latter, looking at the man.

"Only afraid, that's all," said the man, still proceeding with his work.

"Afraid at what — at that lad? Why, he looks like a ghost. I would engage to thrash him with one hand."

"You might beat me with no hands at all," said I, "fair damsel, only by looking at me; I never saw such a face and figure, both regal. Why, you look like Ingeborg, Queen of Norway . . ."

A fight and a hard one is, of course, clearly drawn. The Flaming Tinman advances and we have some almost stylized yet persuasively natural dialogue which so characterizes Hemingway.

"Why, as I am alive, this is the horse of that mumping villain Slingsby."

"It's his no longer. I bought it and paid for it."

"It's mine now," said the fellow. "I swore I would seize it the next time I found it on my beat, ay, and beat the master, too."

"I am not Slingsby."

"All's one for that."

"You don't say you will beat me?"

"Afraid was the word."

"I'm sick and feeble."

"Hold up your fists."

"Won't the horse satisfy you?"

"Horse nor bellows, either."

"No mercy, then."

"Here's at you."

The fight is on, and no matter how many blows are landed by the Romany Rye, the Flaming Tinman strikes more telling ones. He has his arms around his victim, hurls him down, and falls upon him. But for fair play Belle pulls the Tinman off, and now she is the second for his opponent. During a breathing spell he sits on her knee and she urges him to use Long Melford — "this long right of yours . . . if you did, I shouldn't wonder if you yet stand a chance." The Flaming Tinman slips, his fist comes with mighty force against a tree, and the Romany Rye collects all his strength for a blow behind the Tinman's ear. By chance this is a right-hand blow, and the fight is ended.

"Hurrah for Long Melford!" I heard Belle exclaim. "There is nothing like Long Melford for shortness the world over."

And later:

"They were bad people and I did not like them, but they were my only acquaintance in the wide world . . . Of the two I believe Grey Moll to be the best, for she at any rate is true and faithful to him, and I like truth and constancy, don't you, young man?"

"Yes," I said, "they are very nice things. I feel very strangely."

"How do you feel, young man?"

"Very much afraid."

"Afraid at what? At the Flaming Tinman? Don't be afraid of him. He won't come back, and if he did he shouldn't touch you in this state. I'd fight him for you, but he won't come back, so don't be afraid of him."

"I'm not afraid of the Flaming Tinman."

"What, then, are you afraid of?"

"The evil one."

"The evil one," said the girl, "where is he?"

"Coming upon me."

"Never heed," said the girl, "I'll stand by you."

And so to a different and besetting theme of myth and reality which might have suited a Hemingway. The Romany Rye and Isopel Berners lodged awhile in Mumper's Dingle but did nothing to make the earth move under them. Shortly he was giving Isopel Berners lessons in Armenian and she, with a "Gorgio shunella" and a "Dovey do," both pure Romany, was proving that she knew the language of the road. I don't suppose a copulation scene would have come naturally in the book, or that it was missed in Borrow's day, or even that it would be much missed in our own time.

With this, the theme of my morning walk may be considered complete, or a little more than complete, since I added to it afterward. Some may think that putting Borrow beside Hemingway is a flawed notion, since Borrow, bearing the stamp of the era in which he lived, suffers that worst of literary damnations, being dated. But I have seen many writers undergo that erosion, and when the critics and criticism of today are ripened, as they will be, it may be noticed that Hemingway is dated too. Dating in this sense is a more rapid process than ever it has been in the world before.

As for Graham and me at this moment, we have been too long away from our trail around the pond and our maximum speed of four miles an hour. My morning reflections no doubt arose from an impulse to flee the cult of contemporaneousness, no matter what its latest symbol. This hour need not sustain the burden of deciding who and what will be the great and greatest. I am now showing my own prejudice, for like others of my age I want to look back upon the present as I do upon the past, and looking back upon it will be the same as looking down upon it. Yet if we don't claim all we possibly can from longevity, what is the use of having lived so long?

I still do not remember whether Alida Gulick's lights were on when Graham and I went past at a little after six this morning, though I'm sure I made a point of noticing at the time.

꿍

A young man came to see me about a matter of genealogy. I am not ordinarily a source of genealogical information, even about my own family line except for recent generations, but I have collected information about the master mariners of Martha's Vineyard, and it was about two of these the young man wanted to inquire.

I invited him into the living room where I sat by the fireplace and he got out his papers and spread them beside him on the sofa against the wall. Forewarned of his quest, I had produced some notes of my own.

"I understand that both Peter Pease Senior and Peter Pease Junior were captains," the young man said.

"Yes. Master mariners."

"That's what I thought."

"But there was also Peter Pease III who died in 1822 at Port-au-Prince. He had been married in 1817 to Sally Dunham."

"Let me get that down," said the young man, writing away on his pad.

Just then Graham entered the living room, walked across to the fireplace, extended himself, and put his forefeet on my knee. I pushed him away twice.

"That's a beautiful collie," said the young man.

"Thank you."

"What dates do you have for Peter Pease Senior?"

Graham had crossed the room and was now standing erect with his front feet on the couch near the north windows. His glance was directed nowhere in particular. The young man looked at him with surprised interest.

"What's he doing?"

"Just standing, I guess."

"I never saw a dog do that. What dates do you have for the first Captain Peter Pease?"

"All I know is that he was a cabin boy in the fleet of General Pepperell at the capture of Cape Breton in 1745."

The young man's attention was divided. His eyes kept veering toward Graham.

"Does he do that often? I mean, doesn't he make you nervous?"

"Not now," I said. "He and I are used to each other."

We were both looking at Graham, and I don't know why I thought of Shakespeare's "he doth bestride this narrow world like a colossus," because Graham wasn't bestriding anything. He was just fully extended.

The young man whistled, but Graham did not glance in his direction. Graham remained inattentive.

The young man attempted to concentrate on his papers.

"Did you say he was a cabin boy in 1765?"

"1745."

"But according to my record the first Peter Pease wasn't born until 1734, so he would have been eleven years old when he was with General . . ."

"Pepperell. I suppose he would."

"I should think he'd be tired of that position," said the young man, referring to Graham, not to General Pepperell.

"He doesn't seem to mind it."

"Why doesn't he get back down on the floor?"

"He would if he wanted to."

"Gosh!" said the young man.

"As to Peter Pease Junior, I have some notes I got from Miss May Peckham in 1954 . . ."

The young man was trying to listen.

"He was married to Keziah Fitch, who was descended from Reverend James Fitch of Saybrook and Norwich, Connecticut, who was a noted divine of his day . . ."

"Just a minute," said the young man, picking up some of his papers from the floor where he had dropped them. "Do you mind going over that again?"

I could understand why he kept looking around at Graham.

I repeated what I had said about Reverend James Fitch, adding that Major James Fitch was a son. The young man floundered, and I suspected he lost most of what I was trying to tell him.

"This has to do with which Peter Pease?" he asked, apparently in self-defense as much as anything else.

"The second one. Major James Fitch seems to have been a noted man, and his memory is honored by the Fitch Gateway in the Harkness Memorial on the Yale campus . . ."

"Just a minute. I'm a little confused. These Fitches . . ."

"His son, Jedidiah Fitch . . ."

"Whose son?"

"Major James Fitch's. He left Connecticut and settled on Nantucket where he married Abigail Coffin . . ."

"Oh, gee," said the young man, trying not to look in Graham's direction.

"I'll tell you what I'll do. I'll write all this down clearly and mail it to you."

"That will be wonderful. Tremendous."

I couldn't help adding one more detail, the sort genealogists usually relish. "It's an odd thing. Keziah Fitch was the daughter of Benjamin and Anna Osborne Fitch, and both of them died as paupers."

"Really?" The young man had gathered his papers and risen from the couch. He couldn't get out soon enough. Graham, still fully extended, eyes roving indifferently, jaws parted a little for easier breathing, indicated no interest.

I saw the young man to the door. When I returned to the living room I thought that Graham, though not relinquishing his pose, appeared somehow expectant. As for me, the experience had not been at all embarrassing, but had been rather on the happy side.

"All right," I said to Graham. "You win. I suppose it's a walk you want this time, so let's get going."

We were soon on the trail together in the sunlight, Graham's plume waving as he trotted briskly, all interest in everything around him.

~

At the filling station I met Anna Johnson, and after the usual greetings I mentioned by way of explaining what might have seemed impolite haste that I was heading for a funeral.

"Whose funeral?" she asked.

"Olivia Lind."

"Oh, Elmer's wife? Isn't that awful!"

"Well, she was eighty-three."

"Oh, then she had a license."

"Yes, she had a license."

"God rest her soul!" Anna said.

～

An encounter shortly before the end of winter lurks in my mind. Graham was well ahead of me on the pond path in the early morning darkness, which was such that I carried a flashlight for use in the black places.

Just beyond the dike where the path twists upon itself Graham halted abruptly, then turned back in the direction from which we had come, passing me at a good clip. The flashlight beam did not quite reach whatever he had seen but in a moment the information had come to me that a skunk stood at a little distance dead ahead. I turned and retreated, though not nearly at Graham's speed.

This incident showed that Graham was perceptive about nature and nature's ways. He had learned about skunks. But I did think he should have let me know what was going on, and even maybe have waited for me before looking to his own preservation.

～

A little after spring had first come, and it's never easy to set a time for that, we had another meeting on the path, this one in mid-morning. We found ourselves approaching a young man and a large dog, its breed rather obscure because of his thick rough coat of curly hair, mostly gray. Graham and this stranger got along well — they were about of a size — and I conversed with the master.

He explained that he had contrived a cross between a collie and an Old English sheepdog, believing that both were overbred and might benefit from his experiment. I could see it had turned out well. Oddly, the sheepdog-collie, though mostly like the former in color, bore the typical pattern of a collie's coat. His eyes were brown and entirely visible, not covered with hair like those of a sheepdog, and I knew those eyes at once, for I had seen the like of them countless times before. Graham's eyes are like that.

The young man's appearance is unimportant, and I should not be able to recognize him if I met him again. But he said that his dog's name was Alfred and that he had been named for Alfred North Whitehead, mathematician and philosopher. He had another dog at home named for Bertrand Russell.

If I say I was bemused it would probably be an exaggeration, but I know of no other word that applies even nearly. Some moments are charged with a strangeness of experience that is beyond logic, and in any case one man's mysticism is another man's nonsense. Graham and I walked on around the pond, past the wild thickets, under a new blue sky in air that lost none of its freshness as the morning slowly lengthened.

I cannot account reasonably for what I did when I reached home. It was not that I supposed Alfred was more than an ordinary dog, or that because of his christening he might be even remotely acquainted with *The Principles of Natural Knowledge* or *Nature and Life*. All the same, I took down my copy of *The Practical Cogitator*, which has several pregnant selections by Alfred North Whitehead, and turned to one of the longer passages. I then closed my eyes and put my right forefinger quickly on one open page, so that it would fall by free chance and not by any intention of mine. A moment later I was reading the lines upon which my undirected finger had alighted:

Reason can be compared to the force of gravitation, the weakest of all natural forces, but in the end the creator of suns and solar systems — those great societies of the universe.

I was not stunned by this result of my divination, but I felt as people do when they say they are stunned.

"Suns and solar systems" — what could my imagination reach out and grasp but the nebulae, planets, black holes, and all the frontier of outer space? Here, surely, was an intimation of the spirit which had sent astronauts and cosmonauts beyond our blue sky.

And "great societies" — the phrase rang more than true. Not the shibboleth of a political campaign but the extension of a concept into the grand scale — of what? Why, the universe itself. Then the impact, the clear and silently thundering message: reason, weak but earnestly employed, the force that would create a world of newly clarified order and nature at last restored to its own. In a time of crisis for the earth, an old, tried, and all-powerful weapon — reason — if man would but put it to its proper and best use.

It will be obvious that I had employed the divination known variously as "sortes Vergilianae" or "sortes Biblicae." Margaret Fuller of the Concord group, those flowering–of–New England people, achieved remarkable revelations through the use of a finger, chance, and a page of the Bible. I say "chance" but that's the same thing as divine guidance.

Mrs. Enoch Arden tried the method in a time of extremity when her husband had been long missing at sea. She shut her eyes and "desperately seized the holy book, suddenly set it wide to find a sign, suddenly put her finger on the text 'under a palmtree.' " But this seemed to her wide of any real meaning. She could not know that Enoch was at that moment sitting under a palm tree on a lonely island from which one day he would be rescued. She understood so little that she abandoned hope of his return and became the bride of another man, preparing a surprise for Enoch when next he sailed into the little port.

I suppose the application I made of the historic device should be called "sortes Whiteheadicae" but I am not certain, for my Latin is sixty years old. It has aged rapidly in this cold climate.

At any rate I was awed by the close appropriateness of Whitehead's words and the strangeness of the sequence by which I had been led to them. Now I knew what it was to be a man with a divinely appointed mission. Plainly, I must find a means to transmit to the world what had been communicated to me. How should I accomplish this task? I thought of a letter to the *New York Times*, but only briefly. I had been lifted up; I could not fall back to the level of the everyday again. For this same reason, and more forcefully, I could not approach any radio or television station, competing maybe with the "Today Show" or even the Reverend Billy Graham.

No, what was intended — so I came earnestly to believe — was that I should rely upon my neighbors and fellow citizens, the people of the grass roots, as the phrase goes. It was as if I had seen a great star in the sky, and I must communicate my tidings by word of mouth to others who would likewise spread the news in the ancient way.

Here I feel that I should conceal the identity of my fellow townsmen, resorting to a device common in early nineteenth-century literature. It was a method that charmed me as a boy, implying as it did that Mr. Jones had become Mr. J—— for the weightiest and most private of reasons. I did not really know whether Mr. J—— was Mr. Jones, but assuming that to be the case I found he gained interest by becoming mysteriously anonymous.

In my present situation I thought of Mr. L—— just down the lane as one who could begin the spreading of my message. But I remembered that Mr. L—— was said to have gone on drugs lately, along with a good many others, and from this refuge he could not easily be recalled.

I thought of Mrs. Q—— but her water heater had stopped functioning, and she was single-mindedly waiting for the plumber, a delay that might be indefinitely extended. Rev. E—— R—— would be just the man for communicating a summons or a judgment or an allegory, but his wife wouldn't let him. She didn't want him to be "involved."

Gray-haired, paternal, and prosperous General W—— would do well for me, the more so because of his authoritative personality, but he believes we live in a republic, not in a democracy, and that we must trust our leaders so long as they are of the right wing of the Republican party. I knew he had never heard of Alfred North Whitehead and was capable of reporting both Whitehead and me to the F.B.I.

Mr. and Mrs. G—— would ordinarily oblige in a matter of this kind and would enjoy a sense of importance, but they were about to sail for a cruise in the Grenadines from which they would return with forty trays of colored slides. Mrs. K—— was confined to her house with Transcendental Meditation, and Mr. H——, a gentleman of intellect, was neutralized because he had a son who was holding down a political job in the state Department of Public Works.

Of course I thought of others, especially J——, V——, and E. R——, but they, typical of a cross section of today's America, were incurable watchers of television. They received but they did not transmit.

My confidence weakened, but I still clung desperately to my sense of mission. It seemed impossible that I should fail what I had been appointed to do.

One name after another had to be rejected, and then at last a name occurred to me that seemed the perfect solution. Professor J——, who was eminent in physics and even by association in statecraft, was qualified in every respect I could think of — except one which occurred to me at last with almost the force of a blow.

He was too old.

～

When I was a boy, people wondered about the Fourth Dimension, what it was, and when — if ever — it would be discovered. My parents and others with whom I heard them discuss it did not think it would be discovered in their time. Yet every now and then some crank or eccentric was reported to have come upon the secret and to be concealing it in a dark cluttered room or behind the odd countenance with which he faced the world.

Speculation about the Fourth Dimension was different from the elusiveness of the Philosopher's Stone in epochs past, because it was scientific, and we lived in what was believed to be an era of grown-up science. All the same, I understood nothing about it, for measuring was so simple a matter, and all dimensions seemed satisfactorily accounted for. I knew we could arrive at the size or distance or height of anything in the house.

I had grown to college age before it became widely known that the Fourth Dimension was concerned with the clock or chronometer, not with foot rule, yardstick, and so on. Most of the people who would have been astonished by this revelation had died off, but at least in their lifetime they had witnessed more or less the satisfaction of one of the great speculations of their age, the discovery of the

North Pole. One marvel at a time — it was a good rule, I now think, and perhaps we should not have departed from it.

Nothing could have come more strangely to me back then than that I should myself rediscover the Fourth Dimension in the modern concept of the space-time continuum. I happened upon it by accident.

Out of time-distance there came to me yesterday a letter from a woman who used to be a girl named Beatrice Blossom, and it spoke of things that happened seventy years ago. It isn't everyone who stands seventy years away from some childhood event, remembered though not necessarily intact. Seven completed decades and some to spare, but in this instance just the seventy — it's a high place on which to stand and look out.

"I remember you all," Beatrice Blossom wrote, "and to this day we use your mother's recipe for meat loaf. I recall hearing about the day she was to entertain the Governor. She finally decided, after a few last minute qualms, to serve her meat loaf, and the Governor loved it!

"One day we were walking home from Parker Street grammar school, you on your side of Campbell Street, and I on the other, and I began to call you names. I hope you don't remember, and if by chance you do, I didn't know what I meant. You flew at me and we had quite a battle. I came in crying with my Dutch cut minus my hair ribbon all over my face. My grandmother and my mother were horrified. As you were about to be punished I confessed to what had started it all. Then I was the culprit, not you. That was the last time I remember seeing you."

Beatrice Blossom was in my memory and always to be, but not that episode. None of it, not even in the bluest distance. I was astonished that she had called me names, and that I had flown at her. She is associated warmly in my mind in terms of childhood friendship, for Beatrice was certainly the only girl with whom I was ever upon easy terms of companionship before the onset of self-consciousness and boy-girl estrangement. The demarcation was sharp in the New Bedford in which I was growing up.

Beatrice had endured for me in a different and casual way. We were loitering in a vacant lot across from her grandparents' house, and our conversation, whatever it may have been about, was unaffected and serious. As a boy I had many engrossing conversations, but not with girls. So much good talk, and all gone forever.

At a somewhat earlier time Beatrice defended me, and I am still grateful. On the way to the Mary B. White School, to which I went before moving onward and upward to the Parker Street School, we passed a stone-cutter's yard on Smith Street just above Walden. Long slabs of unfinished granite were lying in the space between a long shed and the street, and I always took care to run and leap across them for no reason except that they seemed to invite this attention.

At this place one day I encountered Beatrice and a pretty girl named Cecile, who remarked, "That Hough boy always looks so awful." Beatrice, looking me over by way of finding some possible rebuttal, said, "He doesn't look so bad today as usual." Her loyalty was important to me then, and my gratitude has stood the wear of more than seventy years. How much else has survived so clearly for so long?

I now sit back and contemplate the emotion with which I received the news that Beatrice Blossom, seventy years after I saw her last, still uses my mother's recipe for meat loaf. Surely there is great distance here as well as long time, and I have rediscovered for myself, though differing with the exactness of science, the space-time continuum, the old challenge of the Fourth Dimension.

When I wrote to Beatrice it was not to a woman of more

than seventy, but to a little girl with a Dutch cut and an undisturbed hair ribbon.

∽

The other day I read about a man who had proved a case against nostalgia. He had gone back what seemed to him a long time for his evidence, as far back even as the days of the Great Depression. Such antiquity rivals that of the first Peloponnesian War. I laughed to myself at such a view of time — and space. He had found that in those old years people were looking forward, not backward, wisting for a fulfillment the present was withholding still. "Wisting" is an old-fashioned word meaning "knowing," but I use it in the sense of "wishing," which it sounds more like. This man supposed that, the good days being ahead, nostalgia was nothing more than a sentimental hankering after what never was. It seems not to have occurred to him that the good days had already been.

Nostalgia keeps coming up in different ways, and the word has never settled down, rightly I guess, because it is a restless word for a restless something. My Merriam-Webster dictionary, the big one, which I still think of as modern, though I now note that it was published in 1959, defines nostalgia as a "brooding or poignant, enervating homesickness" and also makes some mention of melancholia. The year 1959 is quite modern enough for me but the definition isn't. It has aged less gracefully than most of the words around it. Incidentally, I have never heard but that once from the Nostalgia Book Club.

The attacker of nostalgia should have gone back to the turn of the century, as I well know because I was there. I grew up with the flowering of the middle class, a time of satisfactions complete enough to foreclose speculations about a possibly more bountiful future. Pandora's Box had not been opened, though the automobile was part way out. The airplane had not been flown. The grown-ups I knew were abolishing poverty, improving public school education, declaring peace in the world, and entertaining cultivated ideas often based upon reading books such as *Ben Hur*, *Quo Vadis*, and *The Winning of the West*.

Some people died young, but that could not be helped right away. I supposed that at any given time everyone was the age he was supposed to be, and of course there is still a good deal in this supposition. The period was a lot better than the one I see about me today. More evil than good has grown in seventy years, and the casualties in my lifetime have been more numerous and more tragic than those before the discovery of penicillin and the atomic bomb.

On my morning walk with Graham, breaking a trail through the white and chilly dew in the first rays of the sun, and, somewhat with Graham's help, I found myself defining nostalgia for my own satisfaction, take it or leave it.

Nostalgia is:

— remembering.

— remembering things long ago, or long, long ago.

— remembering the lost, mainly lost youth. "Lost" clings to nostalgia like a burr to Graham's ruff.

— all our yesterdays, with an acknowledgment to Shakespeare.

— remembering when one was less lonely than now.

— remembering the time when one had no money, and it wasn't so bad a time as many since.

— remembering what still remains after forgetfulness, or what may be salvaged in strange moments after the Freudian principle of suppression has culled out so deceptively the apparent good from the apparent bad, or the bearable from the unbearable, and not always with the best result.

— remembering the difference between now and then, and not checking the accuracy of the recollection.

Such definitions obviously are no good. Twilight is perhaps the most difficult though often the most satisfying time of day. The light fails, little by little.

In this present matter the young and the intellectual are the hard-based opposition. But they too remember, because everyone does.

My favorite carpenter said, "I didn't put a new lock on that door. I fixed the old one. You can't buy locks like that any more. They don't make good locks nowadays." This is not nostalgia but is closely related to it.

THE YEAR 2000 has come up again. It keeps
coming up, and the reason why is clearly stated in the book
called *Only One Earth*, subtitled *The Care and Mainte-
nance of a Small Planet*, an unofficial report commissioned
by the Secretary General of the United Nations Conference
on the Human Environment, usually known as the Stock-
holm Conference. A committee of 152 members represent-
ing 58 countries took part, and René Dubos and Barbara
Ward wrote the book.

I am sure the unofficial report is clearer and charged
with greater meaning than the official report, if there was
one. The authors are eloquent in assessing the dangers to
life as we know it on the planet earth, and eloquent also in
the hope that man will exert himself to survive, along with
the planet. To me, the element of hope doesn't amount to

much, for — as I have said already — I have no conflict of interest. What is the year 2000 to me?

The question as to the short margin ahead "turns on whether the technosphere — the world order of technological innovation, investment flows, and commercial exchanges — can also be revised and managed to recognize the interdependence of nations and the underlying community of man."

The stakes are as high as stakes can ever be: "If all man can offer to the decades ahead is the same combination of scientific drive, economic cupidity, and national arrogance, then we cannot rate very highly the chance of reaching the year 2000 with our planet functioning safely and our humanity preserved."

The year 2000 — there it most dreadfully is, a goal or a fate recurring with frightening persistence in crystal ball glimpses of the future. Except that Dr. Paul Ehrlich kills off the planet even sooner, and except that hardly anyone is really frightened. The price of groceries causes a lot more concern.

I have imagined a sort of litany for the planetary gloaming, the steady darkening prospect of man's world. It never really was his, but he took it. The invocations and responses of this litany come from authoritative sources except a few I got from bumper stickers, which may, in a sense, be of as much authority as the others. I am afraid I have brought off nothing that can be properly intoned, but perhaps this does not matter since in the remaining span of life nothing is going to fit together neatly in sight, sound, or substance. Anyway, here it is:

> So the race is on, and by 2000 A.D. it will be decided.
> — *Root for Washington and I like Sonny.*
> Unwittingly we have created for ourselves a new and dangerous world.

— Register Communists, not guns.
The grand and ultimate illusion would be that man could provide a substitute for the elemental workings of nature.
— If we wait, perhaps wiser counsels will prevail.
The ocean may be the first part of the biosphere to die.
— The bells of Easter always lift me on the wings of hope.
The world will survive the environmental crisis as a whole or not at all.
— Superseason on NBC-4 — You're gonna like it a lot!
The natural resource most threatened with pollution, most exposed to degradation, is man himself.
— Too many forces are hamstringing the free market.

I looked into the Apocalypse for a conclusion, and maybe this would do:

And I saw another angel ascending from the east, having the seal of the living God: and he cried in a loud voice to the four angels to whom it was given to hurt the earth and the sea, saying, Hurt not the earth, neither the sea, nor the trees . . .

◇

Retirement is one thing, and going to the post office and finding no mail in your box is quite another.

◇

Some friends say that I am in a rut because I do not care to travel. They say it would do me good to get away for a while, that everyone needs change. I say that whether anyone needs change or not, he is going to get it, and he should have the right to choose between experiencing it at home or at some disjointed and alien spot. If the spot is not alienated, it may be extraterritorial. Sitting under a palm in Florida or at a sidewalk café in Paris may not enlarge the personality so much as confirm the status quo. Even if you travel, you must take yourself with you, and it isn't what you read on a menu in a foreign language that necessarily counts most.

Going from place to place may not be a better form of change than staying at home and taking yoga lessons or studying Transcendental Meditation. More people dread travel than care to admit it. I have long admired the notion of someone whose identity I have forgotten, that he could very cheaply have the advantages of travel by sitting in the attic with his feet in ice water, looking at the pictures in the *National Geographic* and ringing a sleigh bell. Or, I suppose, a pail of hot water would do with a side basin of offal and a recording of Kipling's "Road to Mandalay" along with the inevitable *National Geographic*.

"Don't you want to see the world before you die?"

What a question! Nobody sees the world, and late reports say it isn't what might have been seen when one was young and questing. The world for many of us is best seen from the inside rather than from the outside, and the inside has to be the inside of us. My rut is my own, not a common one, and mostly in my head, as the saying goes. My own idea of it prevails, and Graham and I are able to make secret journeys on many a morning when we have looked at the town asleep.

It is not much good just looking at things while one sits still or travels on someone else's power. Inactivity galls and tends to overweight and antilongevity. What longevity demands is participation, and participation accumulated over a long span of time with as little interruption or remission as possible. Besides, if I should go away I would miss something, as when I came back from a week in New York and found that one of the hangars at the airport had blown down. I regret having been away when it was discovered that the roof of the schoolhouse was in danger of falling in.

I don't like to be out of synchronism with the settled themes of my biography. A traveler's souvenirs and colored slides will not be worth mentioning as against the continuity of one's own life design. Who wants to come home as a small-edition Rip Van Winkle, returned not from a twenty-year sleep but from a shorter interval perhaps as significantly lost?

∽

Yesterday Graham and I, walking around the pond on a journey of our own exertion, freshened into the experience of a new day unlike any other day, were passed by a young man in a track suit who was running at a good clip, not just jogging. In fact, he passed us three times before we had gotten clear around the pond, and since the distance is known to me — half a mile — and Graham and I were proceeding at a rate somewhat less than four miles an hour, I should be able to calculate the young man's speed of travel. Or I think I should. The problem interests me, but mathematics and I are so mutually inimical that I shall not reach the point of doing anything about it.

An interesting thing, though, was that the runner was followed by a Great Dane doing his best with a long loping motion which, despite his exertion, was not sufficient to enable him to overtake his master. The Great Dane did manage fairly well to hold his relative position in the rear, but he could not improve upon it.

A Great Dane does not run as smoothly as a collie. I should say this one lumped along rather awkwardly and did not flow. Perhaps he was in too much of a hurry to flow. When Graham lopes, he flows, and there is comfort in it for him as well as for any considering beholder. He had no idea of competing with the Great Dane, though, or even of interfering. He let both runners pass without comment, as I did.

Later and upon reflection, it occurred to me that I would have had no greater chance of seeing a morning runner followed by a Great Dane if I had been in Jackson Park, Chicago, or Potomac Park in Washington, or Buttonwood Park in New Bedford, or Central Park in New York, all these being parks I once knew, than at home in Sheriff's Meadow. So much for the remarkable. Graham and I at home do quite well enough.

Let us stay away from the world, at any rate as far as possible.

⌒

Thirty-seven degrees Fahrenheit can be a thrilling temperature in early morning if the sky is clear and the sunlight as fine and bright as when a season is ready for change.

I received my ten-year service button as a volunteer observer for the Weather Bureau today. It isn't called the Weather Bureau officially any more, but it is still so called by me. Betty's fifteen-year pin was awarded to her posthumously just ten years ago, which means — as if I did not know already — that she has been dead for that length of time. The two of us over a quarter of a century have kept track of the maximum and minimum temperatures and the daily precipitation, along with notes as to fog, thunder, hail, and destructive winds. We have seldom had hail, but we have had a number of hurricanes.

This suggests the manner of our lives in another and oblique way, and I am glad of the suggestion because it is a true measure, even though the service buttons imply a retirement hobby of aging retired people, and therefore an equivalent long leap toward the grave. I recognize the implications and view them with an open mind.

The man who comes annually to inspect the instruments in the little kiosk in the back yard was a couple of weeks early this year, but the vernal equinox will not be affected. He was busy in the back yard with plumb line, level, notebook, and so on for quite a while, and then we had our usual visit and conversation. I did not ask him whether he agrees that the climate has entered a cycle of cooling, for we are concerned with more immediate experiences of weather.

I have known a number of men and women who kept daily weather records for their own satisfaction, whatever it may be. One of the attainable performances of system, I suppose. I don't think I should keep it up if the daily readings were unaccompanied by a sense of usefulness or even of mission. The Weather Bureau depends upon its volunteer observers, and to be depended upon even slightly tends to make burdens agreeable.

As to those who keep their own weather records over the years and decades, I wonder what will be made of their lives by heirs or executors who, at the end, inspect this history. They are not likely to make much of it, for the weather in one man's life is like the weather in anyone else's in the same circumstances, and what the record discloses is the continuity of a habit. So much living, represented in degrees Fahrenheit and wind directions.

But there is more than one approach, as in most important things of life. By fortunate chance I knew, long ago, Miss Marion Hamilton Carter, a retired writing lady who had written for the old *McClure's* and lived in the woods in a weathered house of old Martha's Vineyard style, which she liked to refer to as a hut. She referred to herself as a Hut Dweller, with capitals, and she ordered her life in a way of her own which was convenient, comfortable, and peculiar only to an outsider. But outsiders were not considered in her life, and had no place in it.

Her hut had, of course, the main house and, attached to it in traditional way, the "ell," or extension with lower roof and narrower width. Our old people called an "ell" a "porch," making for confusion among strangers who thought a porch was always a veranda. Miss Carter's waking life was settled in her porch, at the end of which was a narrow kitchen. The other room, for the porch had only one other, she used for working at her typewriter, meals at a table which also carried the varying accumulation of manuscripts, notes, and so on. A Franklin stove performed excellently to keep her warm and, often, for cooking. She maintained a supply of soup which she called liquid bread, from which she drew when she liked, and to which she added ingredients which kept it in a transition of flavors.

In this room she also played "The Swan of Tuonela" on a phonograph when the light failed outdoors and her candles gave insufficient illumination for further working. Of course she read, meditated, and no doubt played other records, but "The Swan of Tuonela" she regarded as a musical vision of her own life in the woods. Her region was the ancient square mile of Christiantown where the early Indian converts had lived and where she felt she lived on after them, and even with their spirits, in legitimate succession. The whippoorwills sang around the house in early summer, and the wild growth encroached more and more upon the space where she had built a terrace, using native stone, and where she grew peonies because she liked them.

I happened to call on Miss Carter on what proved to be her last afternoon at the hut. She was quite old, one knew, though she never told her age. "The usual age" was her way of putting it. Of late she had not been well and had gone to the hospital a time or two to be restored for another spell of work and living. Now her legs were swollen, and badly. She spoke of them in a soft, meaningful tone, and then she said, curiously, as if there were an answer she would like but was unlikely to get, "What a funny place this will be without me!"

She never returned to her house in the woods, and it was a funny place without her. A funny place, a manuscript obscure in meaning to an outsider, the record of years lived differently, valiantly, and to a particular taste and purpose.

I wonder what anyone, even my nearest kin, will make of the place where I live and work when I have gone out into the darkness. My files, such as they are, conscientious in intent but mysterious even to me — will they be better than the weather records I am keeping for the Climatography Branch, National Climatic Center, the erstwhile Weather Bureau? Will any of my arrangements, irregular and distorted by my way of living — and Graham's — be on any easier level of understanding?

Maybe the daily entry of suns, rains, snows, and hail that have fallen in one's life will be enough, or more than enough, after all.

∽

These are some of the appointments, degrees, and shadow lines along the way by which Graham and I came through to the hot, luxurious summer of 1975.

There was that snow in March, nothing as compared to our blizzards in the old winters, but novel after a succession of almost snowless seasons. To hear the crunch of snow in the early morning was the repetition of an old rhyme, though the sound now was different and less frequent. No more the wheels of milk wagons or drays or carriages. Footsteps in the snow, yes, but the crunch has been brought up to date and therefore it lacks something. Graham and I made up for the lack as well as we could by breaking out the path around the pond. Graham rolled in the snow.

At 4:20 on the morning of April 27, long before dawn, a robin sang in the moonlight. I know, because Graham wanted to go out, and as we went downstairs every window was reflected on the floor by the moonlight. I would almost have stayed up with Graham and the robin, but at my age one does not do that sort of thing. One has follies of a different and probably less rewarding sort.

As the month ended, Sheriff's Meadow Pond reeked as if it were giving forth plumes and veils of smoke. The reek disappeared as the temperature climbed swiftly upward from thirty degrees. I met Len Hendrickson on Main Street, no one else about, and he said, "Morning, Henry. Made ice at my house last night." I said, "Yes, it went to thirty at my place." Such exchanges are in the seasonal measure of all early springs and early winters.

Daffodils bloomed early, and the pinkletinks piped earlier than I had ever heard them. To non-Vineyarders they are spring peepers or hyla crucifer, once called hyla Pickeringii, but our onomatopoetic name runs back to the early days of the Island. The white frosts, winter grasses starched with shiny rime, appeared as looked for, signaling an end of winter — but in wishful thinking, mostly.

Early morning fogs in May regulated our temperature against our chosen interests. Spring temperatures could rise on the mainland, not interfered with, but when they rose on the Island they generated fogs which impeded further rising or even set them back again. Professor Shaler of Harvard, who wrote of Martha's Vineyard in the long-ago, said that the Island had Old World springs, starting well ahead of Boston, but experiencing arrests that seemed like retardations. They still do.

But at the end of May a new warmth triumphed. The sun became hot as well as bright in a blue sky, and the day's temperature rose to 82 degrees. The hottest May experience ever, people said, but they did not remember. There's always been a hottest, coldest, calmest, or windiest in the far past. All of a sudden — summer in May — and while it lasted I must go swimming. Not Graham, but he waded to the depth of his knees and barked.

The swimming did not amount to much — a plunge or two, and a few strokes in chilly water that livened every nerve and inch of skin. Then it was accomplished, the first May plunge of my adult life, or have I forgotten? The earliest my brother and I swam as boys was on Memorial Day, May 30, but not always then. Twenty minutes after I was at home and dressed again, the wind changed and the temperature dropped. So by the narrow margin of twenty minutes I had reached a summit of experience and, of course, of pride. Swim in May? Oh, yes, I did.

Another day while May lasts. The temperature rises to 81 degrees under a hot sun, and I swim again, a few more strokes this time than before, and the invigoration is a greater triumph. Briskly home with Graham in joyful belief, false of course, and not much more than momentary, that spring has really come. Now I will go swimming every day until fall — but no, I will not. Those fogs and arrests and retardations recur. Nature withdraws her invitation.

I heard a catbird singing at Starbuck's Neck on May 10, but where has he been since then? As an act of faith I buy a box of currants at Brandy Harrison's market, knowing that our own catbirds will be at my kitchen window-sill to be fed from my hand. Soon, but not quite yet. The tryst is an old one, kept in May for more years than I can count. The thermometer in the Weather Bureau kiosk shows a reading in the low thirties, and again the pond reeks so that Graham and I take the temperature again at 7:30 and it has risen to 47. The dew is shining and amply wet, drenching my shoes, socks, and trouser legs.

May and June, a round of daily impatient waiting. But the town is strangely alive, people in the streets, as many as we once expected in summer. Growth. Our population is on the march. What will the newcomers do, someone asks? I don't know, but they seem glad to be here. Now a sunny morning, idyllic. Graham and I are early out, and I do my laundry and hang it on the line. The gay tails of my shirts hang down among the hemerocallis.

⌒

I never wanted to live dangerously as so many say they do, but now I must, for I am seventy-eight years old. Going on seventy-nine, and too soon.

I spend my money, all that comes in, and have a pretty good time. Money had to be incidental to me in my youth because I had so little of it. Other things were necessarily of immediate concern. Now I choose to make it incidental, and I can do so because enough of it arrives by mail to keep me going. I don't have to hoard, and hoarding is what I would do least well.

As for thrift, it was long ago outdistanced in our society. The message that comes through most clearly even in savings bank advertising is that of the quick buck. There's plenty of language about savings, but the invitation to get a lot of things free has an opposite meaning. Lotteries, condemned in my youth, are now a sustenance of the body politic, and nobody cares whose undoing they may be. Betting on horse races is made convenient as it never was before, and all sorts of lucky numbers are announced over television and in the newspapers. Money is more important than morals, and it would not surprise me if New York City bought into some of the more prosperous whorehouses.

I am glad to have lived so much of my life in advance of this low time. I have my private affair with annuities and with the governmental arrangement known as Social Security. I feel that I am being paid for having lived so long, and therefore that my years have had a market value I never considered at the time. This is not the theory of Social Security, but it is mine. The Chamber of Commerce of the United States is against it, and I wonder how many of its members grudge the money which, if they could get it, might go in bribes to foreign governments to stimulate the life of trade.

〜

I have learned never to be sure of anything, not even of my own name, for in these days — who knows? — it may have been changed overnight. Or translated into digits. Yet there are some things I will stick to until my dying day, given the ordinary awareness to do so. This may be known as carrying water on both shoulders — and here is the point — without spilling a drop.

I think that in my lifetime so far I have never lost anything by being polite. I haven't always succeeded by any means, but in general I have tried. I have lost advantage and self-esteem when losing my temper, but a few times I have gained a great deal. I think the odds must be different for different people, and everyone must figure them for himself.

〜

Manuel Jordan's barbershop has been closed for several months now. He had gone into nominal retirement long ago after a career touching generations and their style and manners, and his son George was in charge of the shop, but come nine-thirty or mid-morning Manuel would appear, take his chair in a corner, and help out whenever customers would otherwise be waiting. Then George, a good friend and good barber, died unexpectedly, and Manuel was back again just as in former times. Business wasn't brisk in this epoch of long hair but there were old customers who preferred their own way and who relied upon Manuel.

Then one day the shop didn't open. Soon the barber chairs had been taken out. Only a few bare, forlorn fixtures remained. No more the familiar chairs in which customers tilted back against the wall while chatting and waiting their turn, or just enjoying the easy warmth; no more that array of bottles — Zepp's Dandruff Cure, Lucky Tiger, Noonan's something-or-other, bay rum, witch hazel. All gone, and a cold bareness without an awakening sound. From the street you couldn't see the back room, but you knew no cribbage game was going on there.

I tried to feel that some ghosts were left, but I think they had gone first of all. Those familiar figures of the town who talked of shellfishing, town events, Red Sox scores, and the weather — fading memories already.

A town without a barber shop is not a small town any longer. It must have grown so that other social centers have come in for otherwise the barber shop could not have been spared. Only increased size, affluence, and enterprise could allow a town to survive without that traditional male clearing-house of democracy and shared interests. Common man's common manhood — that was the image of a town's barber shop; but I must add, old style, for civilization has changed and is changing.

A man came to see me the other day to ask what I thought of the future of the country weekly. I couldn't speak highly enough of it. I referred to the large and increasing circulation of the *Gazette* and its obviously important advertising patronage. I recalled how Betty and I had arrived in the spring of 1920 and our predecessor, the Old Editor, had told us with a meaningful smile, "I always say that we *print* 600 copies." By 1940, a milestone year I happen to remember, we could claim a real circulation of more than 3,000. And now the press was turning out more than 11,000, with no slowing down in sight.

I spoke of other weeklies too, and the advantage they had in a time of decentralization and the decay of inner cities. So I commended the future of the weekly — its health robust, its field secure, and its traditional relationships of greater importance than ever.

But after the man had gone, I thought that what was missing from the scene and would not come again was smallness. A lot of people don't know what smallness is, and would not recognize it if they saw it.

Smallness in a town, for one thing, is identified with cutting crosslots. Can you cut crosslots to get where you are going? I recall going somewhere once with Captain Tony Silva, and we didn't follow a straight line, even when we had to straddle across fences and nip in back of houses or over lawns. We were on some kind of a committee together, and therefore on official business, but that wasn't what made the difference. The town had not yet deteriorated into too much size and formality. Hay has now been replaced with grass, and you are expected to keep off it. Streams of traffic suck you into them, and they are what you follow.

Smallness. I know what it used to be.

Roger Allen, one of the ablest of contractors, agreed to build a house for a summer visitor and was asked if he could have it completed by March. "Not without I import labor," he said. "Where would you have to import it from?" was the next question. "From West Tisbury," said Mr. Allen. He was standing with his client in Chilmark, and there lay West Tisbury, inseparable so far as any eye could see from its shape and manner — the same rolling hills and pastures, the same countryside. What was not the same was a heritage of more than three hundred years. I say this cuts to the heart of smallness.

A newcomer watched a Chilmark man building a wall, stone on stone, all rough and of different sizes as they had been gathered from hillsides where the glacier left them. The top of the wall formed a straight line, yet the wall-builder was using no measure. This being so, the newcomer asked how the height of the wall was kept so remarkably even. "I build it to my second shirt button," the builder said. Smallness again, one of the ways of our old, small times.

Someone asked Will Mayhew what he thought of the new library. He said, "I haven't seen the old one yet." If he sounded a little grumpy, and very likely he did, it was because the question was an idle one. Will lived on the south side of town, and when he went to his hardware shop he was still a couple of blocks south of the library. The routine of his long life, until at last he locked the shop doors and went to the hospital, was to keep business hours, return home for dinner and supper, and walk downtown in the evening to provide light and warmth for a gathering of fellow townsmen who smoked and talked or just sat, occasionally spitting into the stove. In big places you prowl and explore; in small places you stay put. You do if that certain small-town strain runs through the habit of your life.

A few years ago a Mr. Peters, a summer man, wanted electric wiring installed in an addition to his country house. He wrote to three contractors asking for bids. Two of the three replied, and one didn't. Mr. Peters waited a while and then gave the job to the low bidder. Shortly a letter came from the third contractor, the one who hadn't replied, with this complaint: "Every time you have some fussy, no-account job, you call on me, but when you have a big job you don't give me a chance." Mr. Peters wrote back, pointing out that he had indeed asked for a bid, and that he had waited two months, during which the complaining contractor had not responded, before giving out the contract. The complaining contractor wrote again: "I still think you're unfair. You didn't tell me you were in a hurry." Smallness has its own understandings.

One of the best outdoor contractors I have ever known has more work than he can do. He builds roads and foundations, plants and harvests, mends and replaces, resolves any difficulties imposed by nature that anyone wants resolved. But he can't do by any means all that is asked of him, and he is sometimes considered to be behind in his work, which he takes in order, allowing for weather and such necessary prospects. So, when customers or clients press him beyond the point of comfort, he tells 'em to go to hell.

Smallness of ourselves and the life around us. But some may say that there is more here of the archaic and the outlived than of any matter of scale. It would be hard to tell nowadays when smallness can hardly ever be examined naturally except in the past. I know that city neighborhoods also have their scales of value and their niceties of behavior. But when I look at smallness I see it as an expression of an inseparable local tradition and of individual character that pales and erodes with modern growth.

KEEP CHAIRS
OFF YELLOW
AREA

WHAT HAS CHANGED most obviously in the life around me in my years so far may well come under the head of sophistication. We, or most of us, always were sophisticated, but what a difference!

I am one of those still surviving who said in early youth, "Twenty-three, skidoo" and had no doubt of this expression's complete worldliness. It hardly has any such connotation for social historians today. I also advanced through the stages of "I should worry" — as for instance, "I should worry and get a face like a ploughed field" — and its sequel, "Ish kabibble," and I was alive and growing up when it was sophisticated wit for any boy to say to another boy, or to an adult if he could get away with it, "Your ass is out."

Traveling salesmen, "drummers" of the past, were a principal transmitting medium of sophistication, not only

in language but in dress and politics. Now we have television and what is left of radio's influence, with the result
that sophistication is instant and the same everywhere. I
don't think it is based upon a deeper or broader culture, or
upon any advance in understanding. Its authority rests on
the fact of its universality, and I wonder if sophistication
of this manufactured sort does not amount in the end to a
greater naiveté. In any event, I would be better satisfied
with the transmitting medium of the drummers and horse
traders I once knew than with electronics.

Another aspect of the sophistication we used to have may
be examined in contrast with the artlessness characteristic
of those times also. Here I look back obliquely rather than
directly, and I think the side view is often the more revealing. For instance, I remember — from a photograph — all
the parasols over the heads of the Episcopalian ladies at
the cornerstone ceremony of St. Andrew's by the Sea in the
late nineties. A parasol raised to the sun of heaven is an
affecting sign of long ago.

Once at a summer evening program of the Want-to-
Know Club, a woman's club which has had an extraor-
dinarily long life, the refreshments consisted of segments
of tangerine oranges and ice water.

The *Gazette*'s Tisbury reporter back in the twenties —
and that's not so long ago, either — was a lady of some
elegance. She was gathering notes about social activities
and found occasion to inquire of a visiting acquaintance,
"Is it still Miss Dexter?" "Miss Dexter, but never still,"
was the lively reply. What got into the *Gazette* the following Friday was: "Miss Dexter, but not always to be." Art-
fulness, real or affected, could be thin ice to skate upon.

∽

Suddenly I decided to plant a vegetable garden, the first
in many years. The suddenness came with a day of spring-

time recognition, mildness earlier than usual, air of a frail sweetness, and my surprised discovery that the soil where our World War II garden yielded good vegetables was friable. Every garden expert talks to you about friable soil. The word to some of us sounds a natural alert.

I had already experienced springtime impulses comparable to a revival of religion. I had been doing a little amateur road work, wheeling stuff around in a wheelbarrow from here to there until my back hurt. Then I waited until it stopped hurting, and pushed the wheelbarrow again. The exercise and treatment was successful, and I was therefore prepared to push a spade into the soil and turn the fresh-scented friable earth.

The spading gave me a sort of elation, and my garden became larger in ambition and initial size. Already I was planning for at least two successive plantings of corn and three kinds of squash. Then Dick Harper looked over the fence and said he had a Rototiller and would come around and rototill my garden. This was a happy development and accounted in large measure for the success of my venture. Dick gave me a generous load of that rare commodity, well-rotted manure, which goes in all the books in companionship with friable soil.

I raked and raked my well-tilled friable soil, and decided to put my seeds in early. The old-timers had believed in early planting, and when I was a boy we had always practiced it through a kind of necessity. April 19 was a Massachusetts holiday, Patriot's Day, on account of Concord and Lexington, and my brother and I were out of school long enough for the family to get to Fish Hook, where, naturally, we had our garden. There wouldn't be another such interlude until the Memorial Day holiday, May 30, and so we put seeds in the ground when the daffodils bloomed and the pinkletinks piped, and I am afraid we put them in sometimes when the soil was not yet friable.

Almost always they came up, and almost always we had a pretty good lot of flowers and vegetables.

We were dependent upon rainfall. If it didn't rain, the cistern went dry, and then we had no water for ourselves or the garden either, and had to bring it in buckets from a distance. Our neighbor and friend, Mayhew G. Norton, of old Vineyard lineage, farmed his land, kept cows, and performed many other tasks, mostly skilled. I remember times when he called on us and we all sat around waiting for rain.

Now, of course, I have a hose, and only laziness can deprive garden and grounds of watering. But in my new garden I exercised a lot of opportunism. The corn and squashes I planted because they were easy to grow and, after the first phase, would need no weeding. I planted plenty of tomatoes so that I could avoid the chore of tying the plants to stakes, letting them sprawl as they liked, confident that after spoilage and a generous allowance for the birds, I would have enough for myself. And so it turned out.

I planted potatoes because there were some sprouted ones in a cupboard which I had forgotten to throw out. The books say sternly, if I understand them, that one should be sure to buy seed potatoes, but my cast-offs did well. I saw the first potato bugs that I could remember since I was a boy — two of them — and it was almost with regret that I crushed them. My new potatoes were ready early in the summer and were delicious. I gave most of them away because I prefer to eat out rather than cook for myself at home.

My corn gave me little trouble. A few weedings sufficed, and then the sun came on strong. Henry Thoreau said that at Walden he grew like corn in the night. I say that my corn grew like Henry Thoreau but my impression was that it grew mostly by day. All the corn on Martha's Vineyard was afflicted with pests, mostly I guess with corn earworm, for that was what afflicted mine. Years ago when I had a garden I went from cornstalk to cornstalk with forceps and pulled out the worms before they could do much damage. I didn't do that this year, I guess because of slackness in my contemplative time of life. Anyway, the corn was sweet and delicious, and only the ends of the ears had to be cut off. Of course the second planting caught up with the first, and all was ready at once.

My horticultural breakthrough came with my choice of three kinds of squashes, the old crookneck remembered in boyhood, acorn, and a variety I read about in Blair & Ketchum's *Country Journal*, named there as spaghetti squash. By luck I found it listed in a seed catalogue as vegetable spaghetti. One packet of fifteen seeds cost fifty cents, yet from this small number I harvested at least a hundred spaghetti squashes and probably many more.

I knew that different kinds of squashes would mingle, and the seed catalogue warned me again, but I suited my own convenience in a small garden that did not admit of much separation. As the summer wore on I discovered that my acorn squash plants were bearing vegetable spaghetti. Everyone pronounced the result delicious. No complaint anywhere. The spaghetti squash is something like a honey-dew melon in shape and color (no other resemblance), but smaller. As I walked about in the garden of a bright early morning, I could fancy that some fabulous bird, even maybe the roc of the Arabian Nights, had been laying eggs under the squash leaves. I am able to report that vegetable spaghetti is a dominant strain, and that a fifty-cent packet of fifteen seeds, in marriage with acorn squash plants, will yield almost uncountable spaghetti squashes, even as a horn of plenty. I don't think I will miss the acorn squashes

— I did get a few from a late planting — and having all that vegetable spaghetti was a lot more fun.

Gardening proved good for me, even if I surrendered too soon to the temptations of a hot summer, the kind we had when I was a boy. I visited the garden in the early morning, and the rest of the day my concerns were elsewhere.

Graham and I rose at five, the sun already appearing high above Cape Pogue, the grass and herbage shining with dew, the air alive with that remembered elixir of summer. We made our pilgrimage to the lighthouse by way of Bob Brown's wild moor. Often in July the earliness would be secretive under fog which "burned off" well before noon.

How swiftly July and August went! Many afternoons I swam in Vineyard Sound, and in August picnicked with friends on the ocean shore. The time seemed to be standing still, but all the while it was going, going, going.

〜

I said to Tom Chase, who is of college age, "I remember your grandfather, Judge Chase."

"No," he said, "that was my great grandfather."

〜

Setting out around the pond path, I found myself ruminating about the literary and nonliterary concupiscence of Edmund Wilson. When I read a review of a volume of his letters and journals the previous evening, it had struck me as remarkable that so much emphasis was put upon the matter of sex. He was one of the foremost literary critics of his time, a long, important time indeed, and one as old as I, grounded in an earlier tradition, expected an image of dignity and learning. I had not expected to be informed so readily of his tumescence.

But now I reflected, passing under the arching branches where the path becomes a green-shaded tunnel, the subject had grown from Wilson's own writings. He had, as we say, asked for it. He must have been unusually candid or unusually engrossed in his sexual experience. Yes, and prowess.

Though the critic is ideally as near a universal man as he can become, and though he is, as Dr. Talcott Williams once suggested to me, like the priest at the altar standing between the living and the dead, he is also human and more importantly contemporary than in early epochs. If this were not so, how could he make his judgments in the sharpened context of the late twentieth century? Max Eastman used to speak of "Bunny" Wilson, as I suppose all Wilson's friends did, and this nickname might well have more than one connotation.

Graham and I were on the dike, standing a minute or two to view the prospect across John Butler's Mud Hole, the Eel Pond, and Nantucket Sound. The Cape hardly showed at all in the early haze, and I guessed it would hardly show all day.

I thought of what Archibald MacLeish had written about our strong reversion to adolescence in what passes for our culture, and the smartiness of our concentration on sexuality. I couldn't remember just how he had put it.

I myself attributed the culture as a whole, sexuality included, to urbanization and a constant erosion of privacy. The trouble with marriage might well be that it isn't needed anymore and that it has such stiff competition in the tight places of city blocks. When lives are private in the sense they were during my youth, sexuality is also private, shielded from public glare except for the red light districts disapproved by nice people, and the words and sentences scrawled on fences and in railroad depot toilets.

The differences I have lived through suggest a change in proportion.

Graham and I had now passed through the winding path, bordered by poison ivy and blueberry bushes, where last winter we had met the skunk.

When I first read Edmund Wilson's *Memoirs of Hecate County*, the first edition of the book, his tale "Princess with the Golden Hair" included a scenic tour of Imogen's genitalia which got the *Memoirs* suppressed in a number of places. Wilson had gone into much detail, and had even written that Imogen's "fleece," as he called it, smelled like the sea. In a later edition, I had noticed, this interesting comparison was omitted.

Graham and I were back in the lane, heading for Pease's Point Way, and it occurred to me that this omission, and what might be discovered as to Wilson's reason for it, would make a splendid subject for a doctoral dissertation at any of our universities. It is often difficult to combine sex with scholarship except in very special studies, and here Wilson's rather vaunted sexuality would be the heart of the research.

I attended to matters of immediate observation, though we saw nothing remarkable until we had turned into North Water Street and passed the time of day with a friendly golden retriever. On the lighthouse causeway the subject of Bunny Wilson and Imogen again came into my mind, though I thought I had finished with it. Perhaps Wilson had modified his rhapsody about Imogen's private parts lest his familiarity with the smell of her fleece, though introduced through a supposedly fictional character, might suggest to readers that he was what is vulgarly known as a cunt-lapper.

I recoiled from the phrase, the more sharply because of the blue harbor and the gulls exchanging perches on one spile after another. But then I felt somewhat justified by the realization that vulgarity, like many issues on the stock exchange, has "gone public." In olden times private conversation was freer than talk in public, but nowadays public conversation is freer and often dirtier than private talk. One says in the open what one would hardly think of saying privately. I had noticed that blushing in public is obsolete.

Graham and I had turned at the big rock near the end of the causeway, and looked back at the hazy yet sunlit town. I supposed it was a veil of haze that caught the early light, but the white houses showed sturdily through.

I could never use that phrase about Edmund Wilson, I thought, surely not in anything written for publication. Yet, after all, why not? This could be a good opportunity to test the theory that one dirty word will sell 10,000 books — or even 20,000. This purpose became settled in my mind as Graham and I came to the return loop on the pond path.

The decision rested so easily with me that I was free to reflect upon the sighting of a gull, a crow, and a kingfisher, the three perched closely together at the lagoon. All trinities are supposed to suggest occult meanings. But presently a green heron flew out from under some planking, and there were four instead of three. No significance here, I concluded.

⌒

When I take letters to the post office to mail, I must carry them in my hand. If I have them in my pocket, I will come home with them still unmailed.

I leafed through William Penn's "Some Fruits of Solitude" or "Enchiridion" and came across his reflection that "Death, then, being the Way and Condition of Life,

we cannot love to live if we cannot bear to die." I found
no logic in this, really, but just the same a good truth.

Euripides wrote: "Alas! why is it not permitted to
mortals twice to be young and thence return once more to
old age? For in our domestic affairs, if aught be ill-con-
ducted, we put it right by after thoughts, but we have not
this power over life. If we could be twice young, twice old,
when we made a mistake, having this twofold life, we could
correct it." This, of course, is very sound logic.

No one lives forever, not even Bulgarians, though we see
portraits of so many patriarchs long past a century in age,
due, if accounts are accurate, to the prominence in their
diet of what to us is sold as cultured milk. I recall a girl at
college who lunched every day on a yogurt called "Bulgar-
zoon." I hope she is surviving still.

～

For two consecutive mornings Graham has called me at
five o'clock sharp by putting his wet nose in my face. It
wasn't that he wanted to go out. His request for that
would have been made in the usual form of descending to
the third step of the staircase, and anyway he knew I had
fastened the kitchen door open for his convenience, the
moderate weather making this feasible. What he wanted,
I think, was to make sure that he and I were still com-
patible and that the day was beginning as usual.

It was about to make a proper beginning, of course, and
as soon as he had awakened me he uttered a few moderate
and affectionate sounds, then retired to his own room and
went to sleep.

His awareness of precise times would astonish me if I
had not experienced it in other collies. I assume it is true
in all dogs in settled households. They become aware of
fixed appointments such as arising, departing, arriving,
mealtime and so on, and are self-alerted accordingly.

When five o'clock occurs in darkness, an hour before sunrise, and the town clock — which is running slow — has not yet struck, Graham must depend upon some inner timing, or some circumstances known to him but occult to me.

He ate another whole banana yesterday. We were picnicking on the ocean beach from which the summer plenitude of vacationers had receded, leaving only a scattering here and there. We did not mind their presence, for there was solitude enough for all, if this contradictory statement can be correctly understood. Nor had we found the thickly clustering numbers of summer at all annoying. They were a good lot under their beach umbrellas, flying their gay kites, playing with their children and their dogs. We and they were seeking the companionship of sea, sky, and all the bright, warm side of nature's year, here where life began, and where it is good to keep the trysts of frequent return.

The Island's South Beach is broad and of clean washed and driven sand, shelving from an upper line of dunes, its profile often changed as the surf of gales or distant storms eats it away. There is a constant march of sand before the slanting southwest winds which drive it from west to east and finally beyond land's end into outlying shoals. Beyond the clean horizon line nothing but ocean intervenes until the distant coast of Spain where the castles are or used to be.

Before we had our picnic we swam in the gently rolling swell which broke noisily at first, then purled and sucked out again from scallops it had made upon the sand. The air had become cool overnight with a brisk northeasterly wind, a change of weather characteristic of the turn of summer into fall. After midday the breeze dropped, then blew from the southwest, more moderate now, but we were deprived of a lee position.

Graham ate his banana when we were finishing off our picnic. He eats not from one end down toward the middle but broadside on, gorging as well as he can, and finishing off in three or four bites if the banana is properly held and peeled for him, though he would eat the peel too if he had to.

He has his preferred methods of eating. Often he lies on the kitchen floor with his bowl between his front paws, giving close attention to whatever morsels of meat can be separated from the more ordinary kibbles, and using his tongue as an instrument of precision. At other times he stands over the bowl and easily manages the greater lift this posture requires. His heartworm pills I must administer by hand, for if they are mixed with his food he will consume everything else and the little pink pill will be left alone in the bottom of the bowl.

We left the beach reluctantly, almost as if we would not be seeing it again. We won't be seeing it often as days and nights become colder, but we will turn to the woods and on sunny, calm days to the hills and their commanding views.

$\sim$

This morning Graham and I met a young man, a young woman, and an Irish setter in a Volkswagen bus not far from the Harbor View hotel. They had taken a wrong turn when they intended to follow the main road to the ferry slip at Vineyard Haven. They were so young and so attractively lost that Graham and I liked them at once. We stood a minute or two discussing turns and directions and, not so incidentally, the fine view over the harbor and bay toward Cape Pogue that they were glad to have seen in this innocent morning light.

The wrong turn might prove an opportunity, as I suggested to them, but they smiled and said they really must catch the ferry. They had plenty of time, I was afraid, and I wondered if they were secretly a little afraid also. I thought of Robert Frost and the turn not taken, and the difference. But I also remembered from boyhood O. Henry's *Roads of Destiny*, no longer fashionable to recall, in which the poet, no matter which road he took, was killed by the pistol of the Marquis de Beaupertuys. We don't have the Marquis today, but we have a cultural dogmatism just as deadly.

∽

So I did not judge as to the future of these young people but only thought of it, projecting and wondering. I could have no idea, really, of what might await any of the young. I thought of myself as having grown up with the country. But the country of anyone, anywhere, is sure to have been full grown in many senses before he was born. This is a recognizable precondition. All the same there must remain something and, with luck, something special that must be grown up with. Ways diverge, distances open, perspectives change.

I can look ahead only over a vista of the past, a landscape traveled. The journey was not always so harsh or bitter as it often seemed, and I can say this freely now, because I do not have to be young again. Whether the rewards along the way will be as great from now on, I cannot even try to predict. I would not even try to look into the view which for me must be toward an afternoon sun.

"Trifles and little happenings seem dear when you recall you will not be seeing them always," wrote a Mississippi poet, Will Percy, and went on to name his life's accumulated treasure as the jackdaw pickings of a curious and secret heart. I imagine it is pretty much that way with everyone.

∽

Mid-September and I am up at 5:15. Three Shredded Wheat biscuits, coffee, and two small plums for breakfast.

Then to the lighthouse, the sun up, as we say, bright red, at 6:30 sharp. Water light blue with tidal streakings, all tranquil and coolly breathing, though not really. What could be felt was not respiration but the frontier over which last night passed into today. Red sunlight reflected from Chappaquiddick windows and then from the windows of the houses on Tower Hill.

At the top of the walk across from the Harbor View a young man and a young woman clasped in romantic embrace. No wonder. I didn't look too closely, but her face seemed piquant and fresh like the morning, her hair strawblond. She smiled at Graham, who had to be gone back for.

On the way home I relished the smell of the clematis, which is flowering in torrents over many fences. This is the scent of September itself, not all sweetness, not really sharp, but implicit with a tang of summer gone and autumn coming while the sun still shines warmly, off-center in the sky. But I think this about other smells of the time of year.

◇

I always read with promptness and interest the letters in the *New York Times Book Review* written by aggrieved, wounded, angered, and insulted writers taking exception to reviews of their works. I have observed that these writers never get the best of it; the critics dig the knife in more deeply, change their ground slightly and take the writer from the rear, or assume a slightingly superior tone which is perhaps hardest of all to be borne.

On behalf of all the writers who suffer, I can offer comfort from high authorities.

Ellen Glasgow: "Surely, there can be no worse fashion in criticism than the practice of rebuking an author because he has not written another, and an entirely different book, which he had no intention of writing, upon a subject of which he remains, whether happily or unhappily, ignorant."

Virginia Woolf: "Our gratitude largely takes the form of thanking them for having shown us what we certainly could not do, but as certainly, perhaps, do not wish to do . . ."

Sainte-Beuve: (I stole this one. I didn't get it from original reading.) "Nothing is more painful to me than the disdain with which people treat second-rate authors, as if there were room only for the first-raters."

My own judgment is, however, that a writer's only real complaint lies against those who ignore him. An adversary position is a sign of importance somewhere, and may be stimulating, but no position at all is the death of concern and of hope.

I have put by a few other observations about writers and writing because they interested me.

Virginia Woolf wrote in her journal, "Writing is effort. Writing is despair." And she had this small remark about an easy trick that writers have: "Three dots to signify I don't know what I mean."

"The work of writing," James Gould Cozzens wrote, "can be easy only for those who have not learned to write."

Of Wright Morris, Hiram Haydn said, "He limits himself to the ordinary to prove there is no such thing."

◇

I think I have my pedometer accurately adjusted. It showed an even three miles when Graham and I reached home this morning. Our walk had occupied an hour. We had walked briskly with good reason, for the temperature had fallen during the night to 47, and there was a clear, fresh northerly wind. The horizon would have been an ideal border against the blue sky, marking the contour of a revolving earth, but the whipped-up waves made it appear as if it had been cut with old-fashioned pinking shears such as my mother used.

Most people who think they walk regularly at a pace of four miles an hour are surely mistaken. That would be almost a dead run. One can sustain the pace for a little while, but there are bound to be moments of flagging, diverted attention, or just pausing to look at something, all meaning a loss of time. I would never claim four miles an hour. There would be no purpose in it, anyway. All Graham and I care to do is to maintain a good, happy stride. Graham makes side excursions, but he catches up.

Just now I saw a mockingbird fly into a wild cherry tree near the marsh in Ox Pond Meadow, and I hope to see him often during the winter. I think he plans to stay. Two great blue herons flew up prehistorically against the sky.

I thought I had lost track of Graham's birthday, but I have found the record. He was born on September 19, 1971, and will be four years old this month. It was registering him with the American Kennel Club that I didn't bother about, but I am just as pleased to know his parentage. His sire was Kingbo Fanci Pants and his dam Kingbo Golden Fantasy. No need dwelling on those names. It is the genes that matter, and genealogy has little to say of them.

Emerson wrote that "If we look into the eyes of the youngest person, we sometimes discover that here is one who knows already what you would go with much pains to teach him; there is that in him which is the ancestor of all around him."

I don't believe too much in this except as to dogs. They need to bring more native good sense into the world than humans do. Of course babies are likely to grow into ancestors but they will need a lot of qualifying experiences before they will pass dogs and other nonhuman creatures on the journey upward.

The four years Graham and I have spent together have been even more rewarding than I could have supposed. Dr. Bob Nevin says, "Living alone is in itself an illness," and this is earnestly true. I am in Graham's debt, for since he came to our house I have not been alone for one minute without an aim in life.

A tree warden sawed a limb from a big tree in front of a house on North Water Street and the owner, a woman, burst out the front door in fury and made him nail the limb back. I approve of this, of course, but the woman wouldn't have done it if she hadn't lived alone. There are other warning cases I could cite.

The companionship of a dog is far more important than can be expressed by one who exaggerates it. Or who interprets the dog's side of the arrangement in human terms. The value of Graham is in his character as a dog, not in any imagined semihumanhood. We communicate each on his own terms, accept the fact of many common interests, and share certain understandings, but we always live in parallel, with some currents of air and mystery between us. Many husbands and wives succeed with marriage in much the same way.

Our house and yard are fenced, and within this now indigent barrier we make our stand together and comfortably apart. If I leave the gate open, Graham no longer cares to wander away.

❧

If I recall correctly, it was the wisdom of the East that produced, as a saying always true under all circumstances, "This too will pass away." Progress has proved the saying false, because according to the law of conservation of matter-energy nothing passes away. Things pass by but not to be gone for good.

There are some precepts in a modern idiom which I think are likely to be endurably true, for as long as the planet lasts maybe. Here are my favorites:

It will cost more now.

They always fight back.

You can't win 'em all.

Arthritis comes and goes.

You have to settle for less.

～

"At your age . . ." human beings begin saying at an early time of life, and keep on saying it with varying applications as years pass. "At your age you should have better manners." "At your age you should be serious and buckle down to the realities of life." "At your age you should set a better example to those around you." "At your age you can't expect to do what you did when you were younger."

None of this amounts to anything, but it may be said that "at your age" is a universal solvent, though not of the kind sought by alchemists and necromancers in the days before science was born.

I notice that Emerson has a way of stating directly opposite opinions at different times. They are all apothegms, though, and I suppose that makes it all right. I like to do this, too, but in plain language, as for instance: People change. People don't change. It seems to me that both statements are true.

～

I remember a lot of things from years gone by but not usually what people who question me are eager to know.

This was the case when I myself questioned elderly men or women. Once I asked Mr. Spurr, who first came to Edgartown about 1866, what the old town was like, and all I could get out of him was that the stores used to be down at the foot of Main Street near the water, and some of them even farther down on Osborn's Wharf.

Something all of us past seventy can agree on: we had the best of it.

I have noticed that when a planner sits down before a heap of studies and reports covering months or years of research, his first remark can be confidently predicted. He will say, "We need more data." Maybe we do, but we need action too. The perfect world will never be planned because planners will never get abreast of any world.

∽

I got licked again this week on a conservation issue. Dave Brower of the Sierra Club is right in saying that a conservationist never wins. A holding action now and then is the best he can hope for.

You know you have never got anywhere and will never get anywhere, but you can't quit. Meantime, what of the planet? The day for answering that question seems still far off.

∽

My friend Dr. Walton Brooks McDaniel, when he was ninety-four, wrote: "On learning my age they grab my hand with almost crippling enthusiasm, while invoking more blessings on my head than God could grant to his most deserving saint." When he became 104, the University of Pennsylvania made him an honorary Doctor of Laws, and the Mayor of Miami proclaimed a Walton Brooks McDaniel Day in his honor.

I do not even think of such an age, but upon a day so near

that I feel I can almost reach out and touch it — a day I hope will be as bright and keen as this — I shall become seventy-nine years old.

If anyone wants to know what my ambition is for that day, and there is no reason why anyone should care, it is that I may rise at five-thirty and walk with Graham around Sheriff's Meadow Pond and then to the Harbor Light. The lighthouse — everyone's goal.